33254

921
W173K

921
W173K

33254

LECH
WALESA

LECH WALESA

Tony Kaye

CHELSEA HOUSE PUBLISHERS
NEW YORK
PHILADELPHIA

33254

Chelsea House Publishers
EDITOR-IN-CHIEF: Nancy Toff
EXECUTIVE EDITOR: Remmel T. Nunn
MANAGING EDITOR: Karyn Gullen Browne
COPY CHIEF: Juliann Barbato
PICTURE EDITOR: Adrian G. Allen
ART DIRECTOR: Maria Epes
MANUFACTURING MANAGER: Gerald Levine

World Leaders—Past & Present
SENIOR EDITOR: John W. Selfridge

Staff for LECH WALESA
ASSOCIATE EDITOR: Jeff Klein
ASSISTANT EDITOR: Terrance Dolan
COPY EDITOR: Brian Sookram
DEPUTY COPY CHIEF: Ellen Scordato
EDITORIAL ASSISTANTS: Heather Lewis, Nate Eaton
PICTURE RESEARCHER: Andrea Reithmayr
ASSISTANT ART DIRECTOR: Loraine Machlin
DESIGNER: David Murray
DESIGN ASSISTANT: James Baker
PRODUCTION COORDINATOR: Joseph Romano
COVER ILLUSTRATION: David Dircks

3 5 7 9 8 6 4

Library of Congress Cataloging in Publication Data

Kaye, Tony.
  Lech Walesa.
  (World leaders past & present)
  Bibliography: p.
  Includes index.
  1. Walesa, Lech, 1943–   . 2. Trade-unions—Poland—
Biography. 3. NSZZ "Solidarność" (Labor organization) I. Title.
II. Series.
HD6735.7.Z55W3437 1989   322'.2'0924 [B]   88-35346
ISBN 1-55546-856-X
     0-7910-0689-1 (pbk.)

Contents

JOHN ADAMS
JOHN QUINCY ADAMS
KONRAD ADENAUER
ALEXANDER THE GREAT
SALVADOR ALLENDE
MARC ANTONY
CORAZON AQUINO
YASIR ARAFAT
KING ARTHUR
HAFEZ AL-ASSAD
KEMAL ATATÜRK
ATTILA
CLEMENT ATTLEE
AUGUSTUS CAESAR
MENACHEM BEGIN
DAVID BEN-GURION
OTTO VON BISMARCK
LÉON BLUM
SIMON BOLÍVAR
CESARE BORGIA
WILLY BRANDT
LEONID BREZHNEV
JULIUS CAESAR
JOHN CALVIN
JIMMY CARTER
FIDEL CASTRO
CATHERINE THE GREAT
CHARLEMAGNE
CHIANG KAI-SHEK
WINSTON CHURCHILL
GEORGES CLEMENCEAU
CLEOPATRA
CONSTANTINE THE GREAT
HERNÁN CORTÉS
OLIVER CROMWELL
GEORGES-JACQUES
  DANTON
JEFFERSON DAVIS
MOSHE DAYAN
CHARLES DE GAULLE
EAMON DE VALERA
EUGENE DEBS
DENG XIAOPING
BENJAMIN DISRAELI
ALEXANDER DUBČEK
FRANÇOIS & JEAN-CLAUDE
  DUVALIER
DWIGHT EISENHOWER
ELEANOR OF AQUITAINE
ELIZABETH I
FAISAL
FERDINAND & ISABELLA
FRANCISCO FRANCO
BENJAMIN FRANKLIN

FREDERICK THE GREAT
INDIRA GANDHI
MOHANDAS GANDHI
GIUSEPPE GARIBALDI
AMIN & BASHIR GEMAYEL
GENGHIS KHAN
WILLIAM GLADSTONE
MIKHAIL GORBACHEV
ULYSSES S. GRANT
ERNESTO "CHE" GUEVARA
TENZIN GYATSO
ALEXANDER HAMILTON
DAG HAMMARSKJÖLD
HENRY VIII
HENRY OF NAVARRE
PAUL VON HINDENBURG
HIROHITO
ADOLF HITLER
HO CHI MINH
KING HUSSEIN
IVAN THE TERRIBLE
ANDREW JACKSON
JAMES I
WOJCIECH JARUZELSKI
THOMAS JEFFERSON
JOAN OF ARC
POPE JOHN XXIII
POPE JOHN PAUL II
LYNDON JOHNSON
BENITO JUÁREZ
JOHN KENNEDY
ROBERT KENNEDY
JOMO KENYATTA
AYATOLLAH KHOMEINI
NIKITA KHRUSHCHEV
KIM IL SUNG
MARTIN LUTHER KING, JR.
HENRY KISSINGER
KUBLAI KHAN
LAFAYETTE
ROBERT E. LEE
VLADIMIR LENIN
ABRAHAM LINCOLN
DAVID LLOYD GEORGE
LOUIS XIV
MARTIN LUTHER
JUDAS MACCABEUS
JAMES MADISON
NELSON & WINNIE
  MANDELA
MAO ZEDONG
FERDINAND MARCOS
GEORGE MARSHALL

MARY, QUEEN OF SCOTS
TOMÁŠ MASARYK
GOLDA MEIR
KLEMENS VON METTERNICH
JAMES MONROE
HOSNI MUBARAK
ROBERT MUGABE
BENITO MUSSOLINI
NAPOLÉON BONAPARTE
GAMAL ABDEL NASSER
JAWAHARLAL NEHRU
NERO
NICHOLAS II
RICHARD NIXON
KWAME NKRUMAH
DANIEL ORTEGA
MOHAMMED REZA PAHLAVI
THOMAS PAINE
CHARLES STEWART
  PARNELL
PERICLES
JUAN PERÓN
PETER THE GREAT
POL POT
MUAMMAR EL-QADDAFI
RONALD REAGAN
CARDINAL RICHELIEU
MAXIMILIEN ROBESPIERRE
ELEANOR ROOSEVELT
FRANKLIN ROOSEVELT
THEODORE ROOSEVELT
ANWAR SADAT
HAILE SELASSIE
PRINCE SIHANOUK
JAN SMUTS
JOSEPH STALIN
SUKARNO
SUN YAT-SEN
TAMERLANE
MOTHER TERESA
MARGARET THATCHER
JOSIP BROZ TITO
TOUSSAINT L'OUVERTURE
LEON TROTSKY
PIERRE TRUDEAU
HARRY TRUMAN
QUEEN VICTORIA
LECH WALESA
GEORGE WASHINGTON
CHAIM WEIZMANN
WOODROW WILSON
XERXES
EMILIANO ZAPATA
ZHOU ENLAI

CHELSEA HOUSE PUBLISHERS

ON LEADERSHIP

Arthur M. Schlesinger, jr.

LEADERSHIP, it may be said, is really what makes the world go round. Love no doubt smooths the passage; but love is a private transaction between consenting adults. Leadership is a public transaction with history. The idea of leadership affirms the capacity of individuals to move, inspire, and mobilize masses of people so that they act together in pursuit of an end. Sometimes leadership serves good purposes, sometimes bad; but whether the end is benign or evil, great leaders are those men and women who leave their personal stamp on history.

Now, the very concept of leadership implies the proposition that individuals can make a difference. This proposition has never been universally accepted. From classical times to the present day, eminent thinkers have regarded individuals as no more than the agents and pawns of larger forces, whether the gods and goddesses of the ancient world or, in the modern era, race, class, nation, the dialectic, the will of the people, the spirit of the times, history itself. Against such forces, the individual dwindles into insignificance.

So contends the thesis of historical determinism. Tolstoy's great novel *War and Peace* offers a famous statement of the case. Why, Tolstoy asked, did millions of men in the Napoleonic Wars, denying their human feelings and their common sense, move back and forth across Europe slaughtering their fellows? "The war," Tolstoy answered, "was bound to happen simply because it was bound to happen." All prior history predetermined it. As for leaders, they, Tolstoy said, "are but the labels that serve to give a name to an end and, like labels, they have the least possible connection with the event." The greater the leader, "the more conspicuous the inevitability and the predestination of every act he commits." The leader, said Tolstoy, is "the slave of history."

Determinism takes many forms. Marxism is the determinism of class. Nazism the determinism of race. But the idea of men and women as the slaves of history runs athwart the deepest human instincts. Rigid determinism abolishes the idea of human freedom—

the assumption of free choice that underlies every move we make, every word we speak, every thought we think. It abolishes the idea of human responsibility, since it is manifestly unfair to reward or punish people for actions that are by definition beyond their control. No one can live consistently by any deterministic creed. The Marxist states prove this themselves by their extreme susceptibility to the cult of leadership.

More than that, history refutes the idea that individuals make no difference. In December 1931 a British politician crossing Park Avenue in New York City between 76th and 77th Streets around 10:30 P.M. looked in the wrong direction and was knocked down by an automobile—a moment, he later recalled, of a man aghast, a world aglare: "I do not understand why I was not broken like an eggshell or squashed like a gooseberry." Fourteen months later an American politician, sitting in an open car in Miami, Florida, was fired on by an assassin; the man beside him was hit. Those who believe that individuals make no difference to history might well ponder whether the next two decades would have been the same had Mario Constasino's car killed Winston Churchill in 1931 and Giuseppe Zangara's bullet killed Franklin Roosevelt in 1933. Suppose, in addition, that Adolf Hitler had been killed in the street fighting during the Munich *Putsch* of 1923 and that Lenin had died of typhus during World War I. What would the 20th century be like now?

For better or for worse, individuals do make a difference. "The notion that a people can run itself and its affairs anonymously," wrote the philosopher William James, "is now well known to be the silliest of absurdities. Mankind does nothing save through initiatives on the part of inventors, great or small, and imitation by the rest of us—these are the sole factors in human progress. Individuals of genius show the way, and set the patterns, which common people then adopt and follow."

Leadership, James suggests, means leadership in thought as well as in action. In the long run, leaders in thought may well make the greater difference to the world. But, as Woodrow Wilson once said, "Those only are leaders of men, in the general eye, who lead in action. . . . It is at their hands that new thought gets its translation into the crude language of deeds." Leaders in thought often invent in solitude and obscurity, leaving to later generations the tasks of imitation. Leaders in action—the leaders portrayed in this series—have to be effective in their own time.

And they cannot be effective by themselves. They must act in response to the rhythms of their age. Their genius must be adapted, in a phrase of William James's, "to the receptivities of the moment." Leaders are useless without followers. "There goes the mob," said the French politician hearing a clamor in the streets. "I am their leader. I must follow them." Great leaders turn the inchoate emotions of the mob to purposes of their own. They seize on the opportunities of their time, the hopes, fears, frustrations, crises, potentialities. They succeed when events have prepared the way for them, when the community is awaiting to be aroused, when they can provide the clarifying and organizing ideas. Leadership ignites the circuit between the individual and the mass and thereby alters history.

It may alter history for better or for worse. Leaders have been responsible for the most extravagant follies and most monstrous crimes that have beset suffering humanity. They have also been vital in such gains as humanity has made in individual freedom, religious and racial tolerance, social justice, and respect for human rights.

There is no sure way to tell in advance who is going to lead for good and who for evil. But a glance at the gallery of men and women in *World Leaders—Past and Present* suggests some useful tests.

One test is this: Do leaders lead by force or by persuasion? By command or by consent? Through most of history leadership was exercised by the divine right of authority. The duty of followers was to defer and to obey. "Theirs not to reason why / Theirs but to do and die." On occasion, as with the so-called enlightened despots of the 18th century in Europe, absolutist leadership was animated by humane purposes. More often, absolutism nourished the passion for domination, land, gold, and conquest and resulted in tyranny.

The great revolution of modern times has been the revolution of equality. The idea that all people should be equal in their legal condition has undermined the old structure of authority, hierarchy, and deference. The revolution of equality has had two contrary effects on the nature of leadership. For equality, as Alexis de Tocqueville pointed out in his great study *Democracy in America*, might mean equality in servitude as well as equality in freedom.

"I know of only two methods of establishing equality in the political world," Tocqueville wrote. "Rights must be given to every citizen, or none at all to anyone . . . save one, who is the master of all." There was no middle ground "between the sovereignty of all and the absolute power of one man." In his astonishing prediction of 20th-century totalitarian dictatorship, Tocqueville explained how the revolution of equality could lead to the *"Führerprinzip"* and more terrible absolutism than the world had ever known.

But when rights are given to every citizen and the sovereignty of all is established, the problem of leadership takes a new form, becomes more exacting than ever before. It is easy to issue commands and enforce them by the rope and the stake, the concentration camp and the *gulag.* It is much harder to use argument and achievement to overcome opposition and win consent. The Founding Fathers of the United States understood the difficulty. They believed that history had given them the opportunity to decide, as Alexander Hamilton wrote in the first Federalist Paper, whether men are indeed capable of basing government on "reflection and choice, or whether they are forever destined to depend . . . on accident and force."

Government by reflection and choice called for a new style of leadership and a new quality of followership. It required leaders to be responsive to popular concerns, and it required followers to be active and informed participants in the process. Democracy does not eliminate emotion from politics; sometimes it fosters demagoguery; but it is confident that, as the greatest of democratic leaders put it, you cannot fool all of the people all of the time. It measures leadership by results and retires those who overreach or falter or fail.

It is true that in the long run despots are measured by results too. But they can postpone the day of judgment, sometimes indefinitely, and in the meantime they can do infinite harm. It is also true that democracy is no guarantee of virtue and intelligence in government, for the voice of the people is not necessarily the voice of God. But democracy, by assuring the right of opposition, offers built-in resistance to the evils inherent in absolutism. As the theologian Reinhold Niebuhr summed it up, "Man's capacity for justice makes democracy possible, but man's inclination to injustice makes democracy necessary."

A second test for leadership is the end for which power is sought. When leaders have as their goal the supremacy of a master race or the promotion of totalitarian revolution or the acquisition and exploitation of colonies or the protection of greed and privilege or the preservation of personal power, it is likely that their leadership will do little to advance the cause of humanity. When their goal is the abolition of slavery, the liberation of women, the enlargement of opportunity for the poor and powerless, the extension of equal rights to racial minorities, the defense of the freedoms of expression and opposition, it is likely that their leadership will increase the sum of human liberty and welfare.

Leaders have done great harm to the world. They have also conferred great benefits. You will find both sorts in this series. Even "good" leaders must be regarded with a certain wariness. Leaders are not demigods; they put on their trousers one leg after another just like ordinary mortals. No leader is infallible, and every leader needs to be reminded of this at regular intervals. Irreverence irritates leaders but is their salvation. Unquestioning submission corrupts leaders and demeans followers. Making a cult of a leader is always a mistake. Fortunately hero worship generates its own antidote. "Every hero," said Emerson, "becomes a bore at last."

The signal benefit the great leaders confer is to embolden the rest of us to live according to our own best selves, to be active, insistent, and resolute in affirming our own sense of things. For great leaders attest to the reality of human freedom against the supposed inevitabilities of history. And they attest to the wisdom and power that may lie within the most unlikely of us, which is why Abraham Lincoln remains the supreme example of great leadership. A great leader, said Emerson, exhibits new possibilities to all humanity. "We feed on genius. . . . Great men exist that there may be greater men."

Great leaders, in short, justify themselves by emancipating and empowering their followers. So humanity struggles to master its destiny, remembering with Alexis de Tocqueville: "It is true that around every man a fatal circle is traced beyond which he cannot pass; but within the wide verge of that circle he is powerful and free; as it is with man, so with communities."

1

A Son of Poland

Lech Walesa boarded a streetcar bound for the Lenin Shipyard in Gdansk, Poland, where he had once been a worker. During his 10 years at the shipyard, Walesa's willingness to stand up to the authorities earned him the respect of his fellow workers and a reputation as a troublemaker in the eyes of management. In 1970 he had helped lead a strike to force the government to roll back a sharp increase in food prices. The workers rallied around Walesa, but the authorities promptly smashed the strike, killing three shipyard workers. A new government headed by Edward Gierek took over. Gierek had promised reforms, but by 1976 these reforms had come to nothing. Now the Gierek government was proposing its own set of price increases, and strikes broke out in several cities. Walesa had not set foot in the yard since 1976, but his colleagues in the Free Trade Unions (FTU) group, an opposition movement in Gdansk, had decided to call a strike at the Lenin Shipyard the morning of August 14, 1980, and Walesa wanted to be there.

Lech Walesa grew up in People's Poland. He has experienced his country's most dramatic moments. He did not flinch, but participated in them.
—ANDRZEJ DRZYCIMSKI
journalist

The Polish flag waves as Lech Walesa, leader of the trade union Solidarity, addresses a crowd of workers at the Lenin Shipyard in Gdansk, Poland, a port city on the Baltic coast, in 1980. Walesa began his labor activism in the late 1960s, when he convinced fellow workers to join student antigovernment demonstrations.

The strikes were part of a pattern that had grown familiar to Poles during the last 35 years: A new regime promises greater political freedom and a better standard of living. Wages are increased, and suddenly goods are plentiful for the first time in recent memory. Censorship is eased, and workers are promised more say in choosing their rulers and managing the economy. Soon, freedoms give way to increasing government restrictions, and Poles find they have no more power in deciding how the country is run under the new regime than they had under the old one. The government tries to pacify workers by maintaining ample food supplies and keeping prices low, but the government has only a limited amount of money to spend on food. The store shelves begin to empty until demand grossly exceeds supply. Prices increase, and the workers' living standard is reduced in an instant. Strikes erupt. The government falls. A new Communist leader takes power, promising a better economy and more political freedom. And the whole process of reform and decay, hope and disillusionment, begins again.

The leaders of the FTU had watched this pattern played out in 1956 and 1970. Now, in 1980, it looked like a new strike wave would topple Gierek. The FTU hoped that this time the strikes would lead to the establishment of independent unions that would be able to force Gierek's successors to undertake real reforms.

The FTU had tried unsuccessfully to organize a strike at the Lenin Shipyard in July. Then, on August 9, yard managers fired Anna Walentynowicz. "Mrs. Anya," as the workers called her, had worked at the yard for 30 years as a welder and crane operator. A widow and mother, she was the most popular member of the FTU in the Lenin Shipyard. Short and bespectacled, she treated her fellow workers with gentleness and maternal kindness, but had also showed herself to be a courageous oppositionist in several scrapes with the authorities. The FTU met the day she was fired. Strikes had spread all over Poland, and the leaders of the FTU were willing to bet that shipyard workers would go out on strike in support of "Mrs. Anya."

A wall can't be demolished by butting it with your head. We must move slowly, one step at a time. If we rush at it, the wall will still be in place, but we shall have our heads smashed in.

—LECH WALESA
describing his approach to
change in Poland

By the time Lech Walesa boarded the streetcar at 5:00 A.M. on August 14, members of the FTU had already been at the yard for an hour, distributing leaflets and putting up posters demanding that the authorities rehire Walentynowicz and increase wages to make up for the government's new price increases. Slowly, workers put down their tools and began to gather around the posters. By 6:00 that morning, workers were gathering inside the entrance gates for a mass meeting to decide whether to strike. Klemens Gniech, director of the shipyard, mounted a bulldozer to speak to the workers. He hoped he could head off a strike by getting the workers back on the job before they formed a strike committee. As the FTU members began to take nominations for the strike committee, Gniech promised to negotiate all their demands — after they returned to work. The workers were undecided. They had heard such promises before, of course, but many, preferring to avoid the risks of a strike, were prepared to go back to work and put their faith in negotiations.

Citizens of Warsaw, Poland, wait in a food line in 1980. Since the 1940s, the Polish economy has been caught in a cycle of reform and decay in which food and household goods are often scarce. Consequently, Poles are frequently forced to wait in lines, sometimes for hours, to buy even the most basic necessities.

Lech Walesa (center) and the Solidarity strike committee in 1980. Since its inception a year before, Solidarity had failed to persuade the government to respond to workers' grievances. Under Walesa's leadership, however, there was renewed hope for change.

Walesa pondered the prospects of a strike. The opposition had grown in the last few years, but the authorities knew who its members were and could round them up in less than 12 hours. Walesa believed the FTU was correct, that independent unions were the workers' only hope for real change, but he worried that the FTU had only a limited idea of how the unions would work. Recalling the failure of the July strikes, Walesa wondered whether this time events were not moving a little too quickly.

The time for second guesses had passed, however. The FTU had decided to spark a strike, and Walesa had decided he would never again back down in a confrontation with the police, a resolution he made only two weeks before. On August 1, the militia had appeared at his apartment to arrest him for distributing FTU leaflets. Walesa's wife, Danuta, pregnant with their fifth child, had gone into labor that night. Danuta screamed inconsolably as the militia commander barked out the order for Walesa's arrest: "Take him away!" The deputies did nothing, seemingly frozen by Danuta's screams. The commander barked out his order several times, but his deputies held their ground. Finally, Walesa calmed his wife, called a neighbor to stay with her until he returned, and agreed to go along quietly. Walesa returned the next morning, only to find that his wife had already gone to the hospital and given birth seven hours before. "It was a decisive moment for me," he later wrote, "and I swore that from now on I wouldn't let anything intimidate me."

When Walesa arrived at the shipyard that morning, a crowd was gathered at the entrance. Guards were checking everyone for passes. Walesa had lost his pass when he was fired in 1976, so he hoisted himself over the wall enclosing the yard. The mass meeting was breaking up. Workers were drifting back to their posts when Walesa jumped onto the bulldozer where the yard director was speaking. "Remember me?" he shouted at Gniech. "I was a worker in this shipyard for ten years. But you kicked me out four years ago. We don't believe your lies anymore, and we're not going to be cheated again. Until you give us firm guarantees, we're going to stay right here where we are."

Lech Walesa addresses a crowd of striking Polish workers at Gate No. 2 of the Lenin Shipyard in August 1980. The banner above him reads, WORKERS OF THE WORLD UNITE!

Walesa turned to his former co-workers standing in front of the bulldozer. Many of the younger workers had never seen this feisty little man with a long mustache. But others remembered him from his days in the yard. He was a bit of a fast talker, they recalled, but they also knew him as a decent family man who had paid his dues and stood up for his fellow workers. When he shouted out the command to begin an occupation strike immediately, cheers went up. The Polish revolution had begun.

When Walesa jumped onto the bulldozer in the Lenin Shipyard, he set off a chain of events that led to the formation of Solidarity, the first independent trade union ever founded in a Communist country and a symbol of hope that the cycle of reform and degeneration in postwar Poland could be broken.

Poland was the largest and most democratic nation in Europe during the 17th century. Whereas kings claiming to rule by God's authority still governed most of Europe, Polish kings were elected by the nobility. To prevent the king from becoming too powerful, the nobility denied him a standing army. As a result, whereas Poland became weak, its neighbors grew stronger. In 1772, 1793, and 1795, Russia, Prussia, and Austria simply claimed Poland's territory as their own, and Poland was erased from the map of Europe.

The partition powers destroyed the Polish state, but Poles preserved their national identity in Romantic literature and the Catholic church, which the Poles considered the only Polish institution uncorrupted by foreign powers. As the partition powers tried to impose their religions upon Poland, a culture of Catholic resistance emerged. This resulted in a series of courageous rebellions in 1794, 1830, 1848, 1863, and 1905. Russian troops crushed these rebellions, but each defeat only made Poles more committed to their independence. The culture of resistance forged during the partition years became part of the Polish national identity.

During the early partition years, Mateusz Walesa, Lech's great-great-grandfather, came to Poland from

France and settled in Dobrzyn, a region of dense forests and beautiful lakes midway between Warsaw and Gdansk. With family money, Mateusz bought 400 acres in Dobrzyn, nearly the entire village of Popowo.

The soil was not ideal for raising crops, but Mateusz was a good farmer and made the most of his land. He also owned an inn, a shop, and a pub, where landlords and peasants came to settle their accounts and exchange news. Villagers often asked Mateusz, who was well respected in Popowo, to settle their disputes.

After the uprising of 1863, two of Mateusz's sons were exiled to Siberia. A third, Jan, Lech's great-grandfather, fled to France. A chronic gambler, he sold most of the land he inherited to repay his debts. Jan gave his eldest son his name, Jan, and the 50 acres that remained of the family land. As his father had, the younger Jan (Lech Walesa's grandfather) traveled between Poland and France, gambling away the dwindling family fortune. Eventually, Jan settled down in Popowo and raised 12 sons and 12 daughters. Each day, Jan tore off a corner of the newspaper, rolled a cigarette, and read the news.

In 1914 the papers were filled with war news. World War I had broken out. Germany and Austria-Hungary went to war against Russia. With the partition powers fighting among themselves, Poles had a chance to seize their independence. Jozef Pilsudski organized an underground army, the Polish Military Organization. The empires of the partition powers crumbled during World War I. The Germans and Austrians were defeated by France, Britain, and the United States. The Russian czar was overthrown by Bolshevik revolutionaries, who formed the Communist government that now rules the Soviet Union. The Treaty of Versailles restored Poland to the map of Europe as an independent state. The Poles owed their independence more to luck than to Marshal Pilsudski. Still, Pilsudski seized power in independent Poland.

Pilsudski had been a Socialist, but he ruled Poland as a dictator and fervent nationalist. He insisted that "Poland will be a great power, or she will

Polish general and dictator, Jozef Pilsudski (1867–1935). During World War I, Pilsudski formed an underground Polish army, which he led against the Russians. Lech Walesa's grandfather was a member of Pilsudski's army.

not exist." In May 1920, Pilsudski declared war on the new Bolshevik government in the Soviet Union. Pilsudski's army marched deep into the Ukraine, capturing Kiev. But the Soviet army launched a fierce counteroffensive. The Soviets reached Warsaw before the Polish army defeated them in a battle Poles call the "Miracle of the Vistula."

Jan Walesa was a member of the underground army Pilsudski organized during World War I. He often told the story of how he sheltered Pilsudski from the Soviets by disguising Pilsudski in woman's clothing and misleading the Russian troops about Pilsudski's retreat. Such an incident did, in fact, occur, but far away from Popowo. Jan had made the story up, giving himself a small role in his hero's legendary exploits.

When Jan died, his land was divided among his 24 heirs. Lech Walesa's father, Bolek, inherited only a few acres. He grew wheat and potatoes, but his farm was too small to support a family when he married Feliksa Kaminska. Feliksa's mother had lived in the United States, worked hard, and returned to Poland with enough money to dress well and build a personal library. Feliksa's father, Leopold, kept the parish records. Feliksa's family was not at all pleased to see their daughter marry Bolek Walesa. Her parents did not want to see their daughter marry into a family of poor farmers that had frittered away its wealth. Feliksa believed that though generations of Walesas had been poor, Bolek would succeed.

A tall, powerfully built man, Bolek had learned carpentry from his father, and to supplement his income he and his brother Stanislaw built cow sheds for local farmers and houses and churches in neighboring towns. By 1939, Bolek and Feliksa had two children, Izabela and Edward, and Feliksa was pregnant with their third child, who would be named Stanislaw, after Bolek's brother. Bolek wanted to build a new house and buy some more land for his growing family.

Bolek postponed his plans when Poland lost its independence in 1939. In August the Soviet Union signed an agreement, called the Non-Aggression Pact, with Nazi Germany. The treaty had a secret provision for a new partition of Poland. The Nazis invaded in September, and the Soviet Red Army marched into eastern Poland in 1939. Dobrzyn, where the Walesas lived, came under Nazi control. The Nazis closed schools, burned libraries, and took control of Polish farms, turning them over to German citizens. Only small plots like Bolek's stayed in Polish hands, but Feliksa and Izabela had to work for German farmers.

Despite the pact, Germany declared war on the Soviets in 1941, and Poles organized an underground Home Army to resist the Nazis. Home Army soldiers, the partisans, hid in the forests by day and attacked the Germans by night. The Germans dealt ruthlessly with Poles who aided the partisans; nonetheless Feliksa often gave Izabela food to leave under a tree for them.

WARSZAWA 347
NOWA KARCZMA 14
KOSCIERZYNA 22

A Nazi soldier watches from his motorcycle as hundreds of Polish peasants are evacuated from their farms during the German occupation of Poland in 1940. Lech Walesa's uncle Stanislaw was one such peasant — he was forced from his home and placed in a Nazi labor camp during World War II.

In 1943, Bolek's brother Stanislaw escaped from a labor camp. The Nazis, hoping to find out where Stanislaw was hiding, took Bolek in for questioning. Bolek refused to help the Nazis find his brother, who had joined the partisans in the forest. The Nazis beat Bolek and sent him to a labor camp north of Popowo.

Feliksa, pregnant with her fourth child, was left alone to fend for her family. Lech Walesa was born on September 27, 1943. In the labor camp, Bolek and the other prisoners dug trenches and built bridges for the German army. Badly injured, Bolek was in no condition to perform heavy labor. The camp finished its work during the bitter winter of 1944—45. When the prisoners were taken to another site, Bolek was left in the barracks with nothing to warm him but a thin sheet, and he caught pneumonia.

Lech was only a year old when his father came home in the spring of 1945. Bolek coughed constantly and suffered frequent hemorrhages. He was dying, and he knew it. The war was ending, and he waited for his brother Stanislaw to return from the forests. Stanislaw arrived in May, and Bolek held on long enough to hear his brother promise to take care of Feliksa and the children. Stanislaw and Feliksa were married a year later.

As the Red Army pushed the Nazis west across Polish territory in 1944 and 1945, it became increasingly clear that the Soviets intended not to liberate Poland but to conquer it. Most Poles were loyal to Poland's exiled government in London and its Home Army forces. In 1944 the exiled government ordered an uprising in Warsaw against the Nazi occupation. If the Home Army could liberate Warsaw, the London government could return to Poland triumphant. The Red Army, just outside Warsaw, did nothing to aid the Poles during the two months of bitter fighting. The Nazis crushed the rebellion, killing 200,000 Poles.

A Nazi labor camp in Poland. When Stanislaw Walesa's brother Bolek, Lech Walesa's father, refused to cooperate with the Nazis, he too was placed in a labor camp. The harsh living and working conditions at the camp eventually killed Bolek, who died when Lech was one year old.

The uprising was the exiled government's last hope to take power in postwar Poland. In January 1945 the Soviets recognized the Polish Committee of National Liberation as the legitimate government of Poland. The committee was dominated by the communist Polish Workers' party (PPR), founded in Moscow in 1942. As the Red Army marched on Polish territory the committee established local governments in the liberated territories. By 1948 the PPR, renamed the Polish United Workers' party (PZPR), had established its rule in the new Polish People's Republic.

The Poles viewed their new rulers as an imposed regime. Five years of war and occupation had united them in their suffering. Many Poles favored a Socialist government that would break the landlords' power over the peasantry. Left-wing parties had gained a strong following during Poland's brief independence, but Poland's Communist party had never gathered much support. Poles had no interest in the Marxism preached by the PZPR. During the partitions, the Polish state had been liquidated, but the nation had continued to exist. Now the Soviet Union had saddled the Poles with a state that did not represent the nation.

The PZPR controlled the country through the *nomenklatura*, a list of reliable party members who were appointed to key posts in local governments, the police force, media, universities, and industry. The people whose names were on the nomenklatura became Poland's ruling class. The war had devastated Poland, destroying a third of its industrial plants. Poland's new rulers sought to rebuild the economy by nationalizing industries and moving peasants onto collective farms. By 1953, Communist rule was firmly established in Poland. Central planners controlled the economy. Marxist-Leninist ideology guided literature, the arts, and education. Still, communism in Poland was much less oppressive than it was in the Soviet Union and other Eastern European countries. The church, though constantly harassed, continued to exist, and most Polish farms, including the Walesas', remained in private hands.

He was an extremely well organized boy. If one suggested to him that he should try to lead a group, he would be irreplaceable.

—JERZY RYBACKI
director of the trade school
attended by Walesa

After Bolek died, Stanislaw built a stone house with two rooms and a dirt floor for his new wife and four children. Even with Bolek's land added to his own, the farm still amounted to just a few acres. Stanislaw grew wheat and potatoes and kept livestock in a shed that was bigger than the house. Each year, Stanislaw gave part of his crops to the government. He did his best to feed his family, but the children grew up in desperate poverty.

Perhaps because of the sad circumstances of his birth, Lech was always his mother's favorite. He often brought her mushrooms and hazelnuts from the forest or apples stolen from a nearby farm. Feliksa was an avid reader and often read aloud to Lech and his siblings from the Romantic literature that had inspired Poles during the partitions. These books taught Poles to be honest, fair, and never to shy away from the truth. Poles were dismayed at how poorly their rulers measured up to these values. Feliksa was also very religious. She led her neighbors and children in saying prayers at the village statue of the Virgin Mary. Each Sunday, Lech and the other children walked two miles to church.

A division of the Polish Army, trained and equipped by the Soviet Union, displays its readiness to fight the Germans at the front in 1942. Meanwhile, Polish civilians resisted the Nazi occupiers, forming an underground Home Army to drive the Germans out of Poland.

A Warsaw woman walks amidst the ruins of that city in 1946. World War II devastated Poland and almost totally destroyed Warsaw, its capital city. During the postwar period, the Polish government remained in exile, the Soviet Red Army occupied the country, and Poland was transformed into a Communist state.

The children never entirely accepted Stanislaw as their father. He was very strict, and his moods changed constantly for no apparent reason. Stanislaw and Feliksa had three children together, but they fought frequently, and the children believed that Stanislaw made their mother unhappy. Lech often tried to settle their disputes, earning himself the nickname "the village mayor." Lech noticed his parents rarely listened to each other when they fought. One day, Lech found his parents bickering. "Now just listen to me!" he told them. "If both of you talk at once, you might as well both be deaf. Sit down, think carefully, and each of you explain your arguments without getting worked up."

Lech was an acute observer, and he learned from his parents' mistakes. Watching their fights, he concluded that people are too impetuous to have their lives organized by detailed government plans or rigid ideologies. "Growing up in this atmosphere," he later wrote, "I've never wanted to reach a compromise with a world that imposes ready-made solutions while swearing that things can't be otherwise." Lech also noticed that whenever Stanislaw and Feliksa had a major decision to make, they discussed it endlessly, trying to foresee every contingency until they had no idea what to do. Lech decided at a young age to trust his intuition and act decisively.

Lech began school at the age of seven, walking a mile each day to Chalin, a nearby village. He tried hard to stand out among his classmates. Whenever they went swimming, Lech swam farther out into the lake than anyone else. Lech's school was run by the church until 1952, when the government took it over. Classes in Russian and Marxism-Leninism, the ruling ideology in the people's republic, became mandatory. History classes never mentioned Pilsudski's war with Russia, the "Miracle of the Vistula," or the Soviet Union's pact with Hitler. Lech was so outspoken in school the headmaster once broke a cane over Lech's head. He argued with his teachers but also learned to compromise, retreating when the argument got too heated and coming back the next day to make his point again.

Polish farmers harvest grain. Communism brought rapid industrialization to Poland, and many peasants left their farms to seek jobs in the cities during the postwar period. In the 1950s, one such peasant, Lech Walesa, left his family's farm in Popowo to learn a trade at a technical school.

Upon graduation, Walesa took a job at the State Agriculture Department but was drafted into the army soon after. Though he impressed his superior officers with his intelligence and leadership qualities, Walesa had no desire to pursue a military career.

Though Lech was only an average student, he did well in math and physics and was recommended to the College of Technology. The government's program to industrialize Poland created new opportunities for peasants of the postwar generation like Lech. Lech hated farming. "You never knew whether something would grow or whether it would get eaten up by insects or pecked up by birds," he later wrote. A degree from the College of Technology would certify Lech as an engineer. He could leave Popowo and go to the city. Lech passed the entrance exams, but his family could not afford to send him to the college.

Lech was disappointed and discouraged. He went back to school, working part-time in a brick factory and as a farm laborer. He had lost interest in school, and farming was as frustrating as ever. Lech's brother Stanislaw had gone to a trade school 15 miles away in Lipno, and Lech joined him in September 1959. Lech, now 16, took courses in metallurgy, technical drawing, math, and physics 3 days a week and worked in a shop part-time, enabling him to pay for his room in a Lipno hostel. The hostel kept track of each student's behavior, listing Lech as a "troublemaker and smoker." He was taken before a disciplinary committee several times and ordered to stop smoking. Lech paid no attention, though, and he went to the roof with his roommates whenever he wanted a cigarette.

Lech had a better reputation among his teachers. He impressed the faculty as hardworking and conscientious, even though he had to spend his free time working on his family's farm. The students had to sweep the hostel floors. Whenever the turn of Lech's floormates came up, the teachers counted on Lech to organize the other students. He graduated in 1961.

Certified as a skilled worker, he took a job in Lenie with the State Agriculture Department (POM), fixing electric trailers on collective farms. In 1963 he was drafted into the army. Lech's brother Stanislaw was also in the army, and when Stanislaw grew a long, bushy mustache, Lech grew one, too. Lech, a Morse code operator, liked being a soldier and was soon promoted to the rank of corporal. One officer had taken a liking to Lech and had recommended him for the promotion. He wrote that Lech was "intelligent, keen to learn" and that he "would make a leader." Lech would indeed become a leader, but not in the army. When his service ended, Lech returned to his job at the POM.

Walesa developed a reputation as one of the best technicians in the district. People called him "golden hands" because he could fix anything from a television set to a motorbike. POM workers resisted communism by trading on the black market and working privately on the side. Walesa used POM's spare parts to build things for himself, and he did odd jobs. Moonlighting gave Walesa extra money and introduced him to new friends to spend it with. He was very popular and widely respected for his work. "I was somebody," he later wrote in his autobiography, *A Way of Hope.* "It seemed I had found my place in life."

Soon, Walesa realized that he had been resting on his reputation as "golden hands" and had stopped trying to improve himself. He was 24, and he felt he was wasting his life. One afternoon in May 1967, Walesa told his family he was leaving, went to the train station, and bought himself a one-way ticket to the port city of Gdynia. He had gone to the Baltic coast once on a school trip, and he remembered looking out over the sea at the horizon, stretching far into the distance. There were jobs and adventures to be had in Gdynia, and Walesa was ready for an adventure.

> *If today we fail to make our opposition felt, there will be no one to control the increase in working hours, the violation of security rules. . . . The best way of defending our own interests is to defend one another.*
> —Founding Committee of the Free Trade Unions, on the dismissal of Anna Walentynowicz

2

A Worker's Education

Lech Walesa never reached Gdynia. When the train stopped at Gdansk, he got off to have a beer. By the time Walesa returned to the station, the train had already left. Badly damaged during World War II, Gdansk was rebuilt with its sculpted facades and cobblestone streets still intact. Ships from all over the world docked in Gdansk, where ties with the West were strong. Walesa decided not to wait for the next train to Gdynia.

Leaving the train station, Walesa met one of his former Lipno technical school classmates. He had a job at the Lenin Shipyard and suggested Walesa also try to get one there. Built during the 1950s, the Lenin Shipyard was the pride of peoples' Poland. The government considered the shipyard a model of modern industry in Poland and made it a required stop on the schedule of important foreign visitors.

Workers were to be silent, or if from time to time they were allowed to speak, it had to be according to a scenario imposed from above.
—Polish worker at the Lenin Shipyard in Gdansk

On November 8, 1969, Lech Walesa married Mirka Danuta Golos, a cashier at a Gdansk flower shop. Lech and Danuta, as he called her, decided early that they would like to have a large family. He later wrote, "We were ready to accept as many kids as God saw fit to send us, at least as many as we could feed."

Welders at the Lenin Shipyard. When Lech Walesa began working at the shipyard in 1967, conditions there were deplorable. The 15,000 welders, sanders, painters, and technicians labored 10 or more hours a day, 6 days a week, often in the cold and rain, for low and inequitable wages.

To its 15,000 workers, mostly young peasants like Walesa, the shipyard appeared in a much different light. Working conditions were wretched. Painters had to sand every inch of a ship's hull with a small hand file. The workers who built the ships' boilers stood over seething hot sheet metal, wielding 35-pound jackhammers. Half the yard's employees worked outdoors, rain or shine, yet the yard provided no lockers or changing rooms. After a rainy day, workers, soaked to the bone, stuffed their jackets into metal cupboards. They took them out the next day, still sopping, and went back into the cold for another day's work.

Walesa's skills had made him an important fellow at the POM. At the Lenin Shipyard, he was just another number, 61 878, in a gigantic work force.

Walesa had grown used to the camaraderie among the few employees of the POM. But workers at the Lenin Shipyard were broken down into brigades that performed their special tasks separately. The government claimed to be building a workers' state where everyone was treated equally, but in large industrial plants like the Lenin Shipyard, management fostered divisions within the work force by paying some workers higher wages and treating them with more respect than others. The elite workers who assembled engines in machine shop M-5 were at the top of the scale, the lowly hull workers at the bottom.

Walesa was assigned to the Mosinski brigade as an electrician in shop 4. The brigade laid cables on fishing boats. His job was to separate the cables and strip the wires. At the POM, Walesa had prided himself on his ability to fix anything. But when he first climbed up into the hull of a ship, he felt lost in a maze of scaffolding. As he grew more accustomed to his work, however, he became very good at it. Eventually, he hoped to learn enough on the job to become an electromechanic.

During his first two years in Gdansk, Walesa lived with three other workers in a house owned by a couple named Krol. Though his room was cramped, the house had a family atmosphere that eased Walesa's transition to life in the city. Walesa and his roommates were very close to their landlords, helping the Krols around the house and chaperoning their daughter on dates. Mr. Krol's habit of listening to shortwave radio broadcasts reminded Walesa of his stepfather, and Walesa frequently spent his afternoons off listening to Radio Free Europe, a U.S. government radio service, and talking politics with Mr. Krol.

These early days in Gdansk were difficult for Walesa. He had landed a job with a future, but working conditions at the yard were degrading. He earned more than most Polish workers, yet his long workday left him with little free time. Also, Walesa found that he disliked the urban life of Gdansk, where the simple values of honesty and forthrightness he had grown up with seemed to count for very little.

Toward the end of 1968, Walesa walked into a flower shop to get some change. He had never seen the woman who worked at the cash register before, but he liked the bit of mischief he saw in her eyes. Her name was Danuta Golos, and he went back later to ask her for a date. Soon they were seeing each other regularly, often spending their evenings at the movies. As they got to know each other, they found they had a lot in common. Danuta, only 19, had grown up in the countryside on a large farm in eastern Poland with 5 brothers and 3 sisters. Like Lech, she had found rural life dull and had come to Gdansk looking for excitement. Lech seemed more confident and optimistic than other men she had known, and his optimism rubbed off on her. Their similar backgrounds made their relationship natural from the start. They were married on November 8, 1969.

Walesa moved out of his room at the Krols', and he and Danuta looked for a place together, but housing was scarce in Gdansk, particularly for young couples living on workers' wages. At first they lived in a series of hostels, large buildings with dreary rooms and lumpy mattresses where drunken workers fought in the hallways. Eventually, they rented an attic over a hairdresser's shop, and Danuta took a job at a newspaper kiosk to help make ends meet. She gave up her job after just a few months, however, when she became pregnant with their first child, Bogdan, which means "gift of God" in Polish.

By the time Lech and Danuta met, Walesa had already had his first experience in opposition politics. In January 1968 the authorities closed down a production of *Forefather's Eve*, a play by the 19th-century Romantic poet Adam Mickiewicz. It was Mickiewicz who had first called Poland the "Christ among nations," and Poles revered his work. When the government banned the play as anti-Russian, the authorities showed they cared less about Polish culture than the reputation of their sponsors in Moscow. Student protests broke out in Warsaw, and the government mounted a propaganda campaign against students and intellectuals. In March the authorities organized a mob to break up a meeting at

Warsaw University. Student demonstrations demanding free speech and a free press spread to several Polish cities.

In Gdansk the government sent people into the factories to rally the workers against the students. The government's agents denounced the students as "hooligans" and "spoiled brats." Walesa saw through the government's line, a naked attempt to prevent a natural alliance between workers and students. Walesa argued that his brigade should boycott a meeting at the shipyard organized to have workers sign statements criticizing the student demonstrations. Walesa's comrades ignored his pleas, and when students from the Gdansk College of Technology came to the shipyard to seek the workers' support, the workers gave them a chilly reception and sent them away empty-handed. The authorities succeeded in driving a wedge between students and workers and put down the demonstrations with violence.

In the aftermath of the campaign, the government, headed by Wladyslaw Gomulka, initiated economic reforms. During World War II, Gomulka led a group of Communists fighting the Nazi occupation. The PZPR was divided after the war between those who had spent most of the war in Moscow — the Muscovites — and a faction led by Gomulka, known as the partisans for their fight against the Nazi occupation. The Muscovites, led by Boleslaw Bierut, argued that Polish communism should follow the Soviet model. Gomulka's partisans, however, envisioned a "Polish road to socialism," in which Poland would be allied to the Soviet Union, but the party would allow more democracy and free enterprise. In 1949, Gomulka was expelled from the party, and Bierut took power. Bierut clamped down on free expression and began a breakneck industrialization campaign. In 1956, strikes in Poznan brought down Bierut, and Gomulka returned to power, hailed as a national hero. Poles considered Gomulka a Polish nationalist first and a communist second. He came to power promising an ambitious program of liberal reform, but few of his proposals ever got further than the talking stage.

We're not strong enough yet. The time will come that we shall be stronger than they, then we shall act. Not everything is ready as yet.
—LECH WALESA
on a proposed strike
in 1978

Protestors display a Polish flag stained with the blood of a young man killed in the June 1956 Poznan uprising, which many consider the start of the Polish labor movement. At Poznan, 50,000 workers and students protested Communist rule until police opened fire on them, killing more than 40 people and injuring hundreds.

After the 1968 protests, Gomulka dusted off his reform plans and brought a group of technical experts into the government to revamp the economy. Gomulka began a program of "selective investment" to build up certain industries and a step-by-step program to introduce modern technology throughout the economy. He reined in the power of central planners and gave bonuses and economic incentives to productive enterprises. Gomulka hoped that by rewarding productive factories with higher wages he could revitalize Poland's stagnant economy.

In most enterprises, however, economic reform meant Polish workers simply had to work harder to make the same amount of money. Under the old system, workers were paid according to what they produced. At the Lenin Shipyard, for example, workers might be paid according to how many ships they produced. Under Gomulka, workers were paid by the hour, and management set quotas for the number of hours for each job. To cut labor costs, managers simply gave workers less time to perform their tasks. Walesa's Mosinski brigade, for example, might now have 8 days to lay the cables on a ship, even if it had usually taken them 10 days under the old system. If it took more than eight days, they would not be paid for the extra hours they worked.

Gomulka's program had disastrous results at the shipyard. When the yard missed its deadline to complete a new ship, the *Konopnicka*, it mobilized 200 workers to work around the clock. In the rush to finish the ship, the vessel was filled with fuel before the work was completed, and one of the seams in a gas pipe was improperly welded. Gas leaked, and an explosion ripped through the ship's hull. Workers tried to torch through the hull to rescue their comrades trapped inside, but management had cut back on supplies of torch fuel to reduce costs. Consequently, 22 workers were burned alive.

Walesa joined other workers gathering to discuss the incident in the days after the explosion. He met other discontented workers at these meetings, including Henryk Lenarciak, who would play a key role in later strikes. Walesa often found himself among the most outspoken workers, sharing information and complaints about deteriorating working conditions. Though clearly at fault, management never accepted responsibility for the explosion. They gave workers a wage increase instead, as if money could compensate for the death of their friends.

To Walesa, the entire affair symbolized the cynicism of the authorities. Management tried to motivate workers with slogans. Ships were assigned inspiring names like *Unity* and *Workers.* These attempts to divert the workers' attention from the explosion infuriated Walesa. "Human dignity and the chance to be fully responsible for one's own life were not available options," he later wrote. "We were constantly treated like simple day laborers, and force-fed slogans we couldn't relate to."

Toward the end of 1970, Gomulka's reform program reached an impasse. Cost cutting and increased productivity failed to right the economy. On December 12, new price increases were announced. Prices for beef, pork, jam, flour, fish, and clothing skyrocketed overnight. The price hikes could not have come at a worse time, just as Poles were stocking up on food and gifts for the Christmas holidays. Gomulka had come to power in the unrest that followed a similar price increase 14 years before, pledging not to lose touch with the working class. Workers had trusted him, but the price hikes showed just how far removed from them he had become. Gomulka's "Polish road to socialism" had brought the nation right back to where it had started in 1956.

On Monday, December 14, strikes erupted in Gdansk, Gdynia, and Szczecin, shutting down shipyards all over the Baltic coast. Walesa, whose brigade had the day off, spent the day shopping for a baby carriage for his son, Bogdan, as 1,000 workers from the Lenin Shipyard marched to the Gdansk College of Technology to call the students out of their classrooms to join the protests. The students, still wary after the workers had ignored their own pleas for solidarity two years before, refused to join them.

Walesa arrived for work at 6:30 the next morning. The foreman in his workshop wanted Walesa and his fellow workers to stay on the job, but when a column of strikers passed, urging them to join their march to the yard director's office, Walesa's workshop followed. After several meetings with yard managers, Walesa joined a delegation to ask the director once and for all whether the price hikes would be rescinded and whether workers arrested the day before would be released. The director said he could do nothing. Walesa grabbed a bullhorn from the director's office. "What do we do now?" he shouted to the crowd.

The workers responded that they should go to party headquarters, where the decisions were really made. As the workers marched toward the gate, Walesa ran to the head of the column. He saw a swarm of 30 policemen outside the entrance. The police carried nightsticks and looked as if they intended to use them. Walesa was at the head of the column, utterly defenseless. He was frightened, but as he took a deep breath, he later recalled, he "felt something like a great gasp of exhaled breath blowing from the crowd at my back. . . . I felt that breath physically and it was as if I was carried forward by it." As the workers marched forward, the police retreated behind a barricade. Party headquarters was deserted when the workers arrived, so they continued on to militia headquarters where the workers arrested the day before were being held.

> *He liked discipline, was exacting but understanding. He achieved more by a joke and a sense of humor than others did by shouting.*
>
> —a worker in the Lenin Shipyard

Walesa went inside and told the militiamen he and his comrades wanted no trouble; they had come to free the prisoners, and they would leave quietly as soon as they did so. But the workers outside the building had already taken matters into their own hands, entering the building through smashed windows. A soldier handed a bullhorn to Walesa, who told the workers to drop their stones. The militia had agreed to release the prisoners, he explained, and he needed help in identifying them. But as Walesa spoke, militiamen poured into the courtyard below and squared off against the workers. With Walesa safe among the militiamen it seemed as though he had betrayed the workers, who denounced him as a traitor. The workers pelted the militiamen surrounding him with stones. As Walesa ran out of the building, militiamen set off smoke bombs and pushed workers out through the broken windows. When Walesa emerged, he heard a worker point to him and say, "You see, the man — the worker up there? He's failed us." As Walesa left the scene, demonstrators lynched a militiaman who had brandished a pistol at one of their comrades.

Walesa had led his comrades into a catastrophe. He had lost control of the demonstration, and workers had died as a result. Walesa went home, but returned to the shipyard later that day. The workers were forming a strike committee. Yard managers had warned him that he would only bungle the negotiations, and Walesa, young and unsure of himself after the incident at militia headquarters, hesitated to accept the committee leadership post to which he had been elected. Eventually, he decided to take it, but the committee exercised little authority over the strike.

Walesa spent the next morning in his workshop. Word filtered among the workers that the army had surrounded the yard. The strikers lost hope of having their demands met, and a bitter and petulant mood settled over them. It had been an unwritten rule in the people's Poland that the Polish army would never fire on Polish workers. The country might have been ruled by Communists beholden to Moscow, but the shipyard workers still believed

You're young and inexperienced and you'll make mistakes. Don't let them elect you alone. . . . On your own you'll only mess things up.
—director of the strike committee, to Walesa on his election as president of the committee

Poles would never kill Poles. Workers in other shops wanted to return to the streets, but Walesa tried to convince his comrades to stay in the shop. Later, he and a group of other workers, led by Henryk Lenarciak, went to the director's office, hoping to open negotiations with the authorities to prevent the troops from firing on the workers.

The director failed to reach the authorities. Returning to his workshop, Walesa heard a series of shots. They sounded like blanks, but as he headed back toward the director's office, he saw the crowd in front of Gate No. 2 freeze and then suddenly explode in chaos. Workers fled desperately, crawling under a barrage of gunfire. Others were pinned down by the shots. When the shooting stopped, four workers lay dead, including one from Walesa's workshop. "My worst fears had been realized," Walesa wrote later. "Poles had killed Poles."

Workers draped the entrance gate with flags and the helmets of the slain workers. They sang the national anthem, and their voices rose on the words "We'll recover with the sword what the enemy forces have taken from us." Surrounded by armed troops and enraged by the response to their demands, the strikers stewed in a sullen and desperate rage. They shouted, "Murderers! Murderers!" at the soldiers outside the gate. Strike committees were formed all

The Szczecin uprising. In December 1970, violence erupted at shipyards in several Polish port cities. When workers at the Warski Shipyard, in Szczecin, heard about strikes in Gdansk, they too walked off the job. When the government retaliated with force, groups of striking workers and their supporters rioted in the streets.

over the yard. Demands were formulated, and appeals to the West, and even to the Soviet Union, were written. But the yard director threatened that tanks would roll in if the strikers did not leave by late morning. The strikers were disorganized from the start, and the director's threat divided them even more. One group, including Walesa, called for a strike vote but were shouted down. The workers agreed to go home and filed out, 20,000 strong, through 2 columns of soldiers. The following day, "Bloody Thursday" as it was called, soldiers fired on workers in Gdynia. A strike in Szczecin was crushed a week later.

The authorities claimed that only 45 people were killed during the strikes. Workers knew the actual total was much higher. The regime tried to play down the strikes, claiming, for example, that only six workers were left in the Lenin Shipyard when the strike was called off. But the harder the government tried to suppress the truth, the more determined Gdansk workers were to reveal it. To preserve the truth about the strikes became a symbolic act of defiance. Walesa joined a group of workers who gathered information about precisely what had happened.

Walesa became obsessed with these efforts and with the idea that the government should build a monument to the slain workers. Having led the demonstration at the militia headquarters, Walesa felt responsible for the violence that followed, and, during the next 10 years, he was haunted by regret.

As the details turned in his head, Walesa drew lessons that would profoundly affect how he conducted himself as an opposition leader. Many of these lessons were essentially tactical and strategic. Most important, though, Walesa concluded from the December strikes that no matter how just the workers' grievances were, no matter how reasonable their demands were, they could be met with violence without a moment's notice. It was from the strikes of 1970 that Walesa decided that opposition leaders walked a tightrope between the need to secure justice and the need to compromise with a government that guarded its power jealously, zealously, and, if necessary, violently.

> *Popularity is a tricky thing . . . one must not talk but act and work. Talk will not achieve anything.*
> —LECH WALESA
> on his popularity
> with workers

3

The Road to Gdansk

The smoke had barely cleared after the street fighting in Gdansk and Gdynia when Edward Gierek replaced Gomulka as head of the Polish government. Gierek withdrew the price hikes that sparked the strikes and promised an "economic miracle" that would transform Poland into "the Japan of Europe." Gierek thought Poles would support communism if it provided prosperity, and he launched a program to make Poland a world industrial power. The project would be financed with loans from Western banks, which Poland would repay with money earned from selling goods to the West. Poland would also use its hard currency to buy food and consumer goods from the Western countries. As long as the Western market for Polish goods remained strong, Polish living standards would steadily rise.

> *We shall not yield, we want free unions.*
> —LECH WALESA
> at the Gdansk
> strike in 1980

Edward Gierek, first secretary of the Polish United Workers' Party (PZPR), fraternizes with Gdansk dockyard workers in May 1971. In 1970, Gierek replaced Wladyslaw Gomulka, whose failed attempts at reform had plunged Poland into economic chaos and prompted his resignation.

Gierek was a brilliant speaker, a master at exploiting the class loyalties of Polish workers. In January 1971 he went to Gdansk and Szczecin to speak to the workers. Walesa was one of three delegates representing the Lenin Shipyard. The workers voiced their complaints about the government trade unions and pointed to the government's role in the recent deaths of their comrades. Gierek, a former miner, said he understood their frustration because he, too, had felt the heel of Communist repression, having been expelled from the French Communist party for trying to organize a miners' strike in Belgium. Gierek admitted the party had lost touch with the workers and promised Poles would never kill Poles again. Gierek captivated the workers with his plea for a new beginning and then stretched out his hands and asked, "Will you help me?"

"Yes," the workers shouted. "We will help you!"

Walesa remained silent during the meeting, but when Gierek asked the workers for their help, Walesa pledged his support enthusiastically. Walesa's faith in Gierek was unshakable. His sister, Izabela, later recalled that Walesa believed "Gierek was the person who would make the dreams of millions come true."

To reform the trade unions, Gierek allowed workers to choose their own leaders, and Walesa was elected as an inspector at the Lenin Shipyard. The job allowed Walesa to move through the yard, talking to the workers, gauging their mood. Many workers quickly grew disenchanted with the unions, but Walesa believed Gierek was slowly transforming the unions into institutions to defend workers' interests. He argued that the unions should do everything they could to help Gierek's program succeed.

Eventually, however, Walesa saw that the union functioned only to endorse management decisions and that management consulted the union only on the most trivial issues. The important decisions were still made without the workers' consent. Disillusioned, Walesa refused to stand for reelection as an inspector in 1972.

The leaders of the December strike were fired shortly after these elections. Walesa was cited for criticizing the government, but he did not lose his job, apparently because both he and his work team had excellent records. That year Walesa's mother and stepfather moved to the United States. His mother begged him to come, but Walesa refused. "I am a Pole," he told her. "I shall never leave Poland. We have to try and make Poland work." That was the last time Walesa saw his mother, who was killed in a car accident in 1975. She was buried next to Walesa's father, Bolek, in a churchyard near Popowo.

For a while, Gierek delivered the economic miracle he had promised. In 1972 the average national income increased by 10 percent, and wages rose by 40 percent between 1971 and 1975. Gierek's program, however, depended too much on a strong Western market for Polish goods. When oil shortages sent the economies of the United States and Western Europe into a tailspin in the mid-1970s, the market for Polish goods evaporated.

Store shelves began to empty, and factories, lacking spare parts and raw materials, fell idle. Poland's cash reserves dwindled, and the Polish economy fell into a vicious cycle of declining productivity and mounting debt. The dilemma forced the government to cut production costs. After years of steady wage increases, the Lenin Shipyard began lowering wages. The 1970 strike had united yard workers, but the government's policy seemed calculated to divide them, forcing them to compete for extra work.

As the workers at the Lenin Shipyard found themselves working harder and harder just to maintain their living standards, Walesa began to gather with his comrades inside the hulls of the ships they were building. Inside a cabin, they would put a plank of wood over the doorway and discuss the need for some sort of organization that would defend their interests. The workers concluded that they had no more say in management decisions under Gierek than they had had under Gomulka.

In February 1976, Walesa told Lenarciak, the leader of the 1970 strike and union chairman at the Lenin Shipyard, that he was too soft on the authorities, and that he, Walesa, wanted to speak at an upcoming meeting. Walesa's frustrations seemed to well up inside him as he spoke. Gierek had misled them from the start, Walesa shouted. He had pledged never to lose touch with the workers, but his policies simply forced the workers to pay for the government's mismanagement. He had promised to consult with them but never did. Walesa's speech was well received, and the shipyard workers hoped to elect Walesa to represent them at a trade union conference. Management fired Walesa immediately, claiming he had made "malicious public statements." Walesa believed he should be judged by his work, not by his political opinions. He appealed his firing to a judicial board, but the board ruled that Walesa's criticisms of the government provided ample grounds for dismissal. Walesa was banned from the yard.

Walesa was hired as a mechanic by the ZREMB building company in May 1976. His section overhauled old cars, and Walesa showed he could fix anything at a time when Polish buses were left to rust because spare parts were in such short supply.

In June the government announced sharp increases in food prices. Strikes brought Polish factories to a standstill the next day. In Warsaw, workers tore up the train tracks between the city and Moscow, a protest against Poland's "fraternal ties" to the Soviet Union. Workers at the Lenin Shipyard threatened to strike unless the price hikes were withdrawn, and Lech Walesa was rehired. The price increases were rescinded, and the workers agreed not to strike. Walesa did not get his old job back, but in the speech in which he accepted the Nobel Prize in 1983, Walesa explained that the 1976 strike "not only strengthened my belief in the justness of the workers' demands and aspirations, but also indicated the urgent need for solidarity among them."

The solidarity Walesa hoped would unite the workers began to unite the entire opposition after the 1976 strikes. Until the 1970s, the three main opposition forces — workers, intellectuals, and the church — pressed their grievances separately. The church had always demanded freedom of worship but had never supported the intellectuals' fight for free speech, believing that opposition intellectuals, many of whom were Marxists, were no better than the Communist government. Workers had also

> *Man has got to believe in something. If he doesn't, he becomes an animal. A dangerous animal.*
> —LECH WALESA

scorned the intellectuals' political demands, helping the regime suppress student demonstrations in 1968. When workers struck in 1970, students ignored their pleas for support. After 1976 the three groups started to realize that they were victims of the same oppression. Each group began to think less about its own demands and to speak out on behalf of Polish society as a whole.

The church began to defend the political rights of all Poles. Cardinal Stefan Wyszynski, head of the Polish Catholic church, and Karol Wojtyla, archbishop of Krakow and later Pope John Paul II, preached that the government had to respect the people's right both to live in dignity, free from oppression, and to participate in the political and social life of people's Poland.

A nun greets Cardinal Stefan Wyszynski, head of the Polish Catholic church, in October 1970. Cardinal Wyszynski had been an activist for the opposition since the early 1950s, when he spent three years in prison for engaging in antigovernment demonstrations.

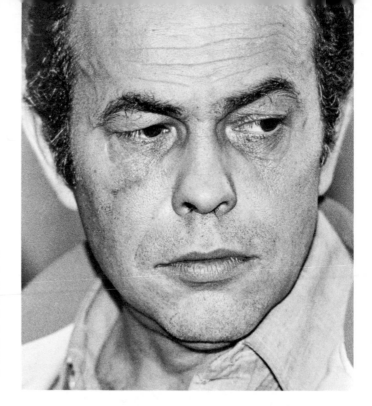

Jacek Kuron, one of the chief spokesmen for the Committee for the Defense of Workers' Rights (KOR). Founded in 1971 by a group of Polish intellectuals, the KOR, like Solidarity, sought to protect the basic legal rights of workers against government abuses.

In 1977 a group of intellectuals led by Jacek Kuron founded the Committee for the Defense of Workers' Rights (KOR). KOR gave legal and economic help to workers fired for opposition activities. KOR became a symbol of solidarity between intellectuals and workers. Many KOR activists were former party members expelled for criticizing the government. They had given up any hope that the party could reform itself and believed that if the government refused to initiate democratic reforms, then Poles should conduct themselves as if they lived in a free country. KOR called on Poles to establish independent groups and publications where they could express themselves openly and publicly. As these institutions grew, they would form a democratic society within the shell of the people's Poland.

In 1977, Walesa began to hear about the independent opposition. In 1978, he came across an issue of *Coastal Worker*, an underground newspaper, and found a declaration of a new Free Trade Unions (FTU) group. Walesa was shocked that the editors had signed the declaration, even listing their addresses, as if the possibility of government reprisals never existed.

Founded by Andrzej Gwiazda, an engineer, the FTU had strong links with Kuron and KOR. Walesa and his mates at the Lenin Shipyard had discussed the need to organize workers outside government auspices, and the FTU's program for independent unions appealed to Walesa as the perfect vehicle to enable workers to defend their own interests. Walesa criticized the FTU for failing to get its message to workers when he first met with Gwiazda, but Walesa soon became a member of the small group. The core members of the FTU — Gwiazda, his wife, Joanna, Bogdan Lis, Anna Walentynowicz, and Alina Pienkowska, a nurse at the Lenin Shipyard — would eventually play key roles in Solidarity.

At first, Walesa sat at the back of the room, absorbing the discussions, and on the few occasions he spoke, his remarks did not impress the other activists. At one meeting, each member described their vision of an ideal society. To the seasoned activists of the FTU, Walesa, whose simple vision seemed to be based on little more than politeness and goodwill, was naive. Walesa also seemed ill at ease with the FTU's open opposition. Gwiazda noticed that Walesa's hands shook when he first distributed copies of *Coastal Worker*, the FTU newspaper.

Andrzej Gwiazda, author and electrical engineer, was one of the most prominent activists in Polish labor politics in the 1970s and 1980s. After founding the Free Trade Unions (FTU) with his wife, Joanna, in 1978, he became one of Walesa's closest associates.

Lech and Danuta Walesa in the kitchen of their Gdansk apartment. Danuta not only supported her husband's Solidarity activities but played an active role in many of his most important political decisions. While Lech was in prison for his antigovernment activities, Danuta made public speeches for him.

Eventually, Walesa became more accustomed to opposition work. He began to speak up at meetings and preside over them occasionally as chairman. He organized an FTU group at the Stogi apartment complex where he lived. As Walesa became a popular FTU member, younger workers questioned him eagerly about what had really happened in the 1970 strikes, and he even began writing a pamphlet about it. Walesa was often arrested for handing out FTU literature. At first the police treated him as a gullible worker led astray by radical oppositionists. But when the police realized Walesa had actually written some of the materials he was distributing, the secret police, the UB, began to follow him.

In November 1978, ZREMB fired Walesa for his opposition activities. Several workers considered a protest strike, but Walesa warned them against it. "We're not strong enough yet," he told them. "But the time will come when we shall be stronger than they are." The following month, Walesa spoke outside Gate No. 2, where the police had opened fire on the workers during the strike 8 years before. Walesa had brought flowers to the spot each December, and this year he spoke to a crowd of 4,000 people, promising that "next year there will be more of us."

Fired for his work with the FTU, Walesa considered dropping out of the opposition because he had no means to support his family, and Danuta was pregnant with their fifth child. As the authorities continued to harass him, Walesa's choice became increasingly clear. He talked to people in the streetcar he took home from the police station. They were angered when he told them he had been arrested for trying to organize a ceremony for the workers killed in 1970. He told them that Poland needed an organization that could protect the rights of all Poles. Walesa realized he had become an opposition activist.

Walesa was eligible for three months of unemployment benefits and decided to put his free time to good use. He went to the employment office each morning with a toolbox full of FTU literature, picked up a list of enterprises where he could apply for jobs, and distributed the literature along the way and at the enterprise. It was a great irony: Fired for his opposition activities, Walesa became a full-time activist paid by the government. He used his interviews with foremen, personnel directors, and even enterprise directors to describe his opposition views. If he was offered a job, he refused it, distributed his pamphlets, and left. The day his unemployment benefits ran out, Walesa took a job repairing electrical equipment for Elektromontaz, an engineering company.

The opposition planned another ceremony for the workers killed in 1970. As the ninth anniversary approached in December 1979, a police car kept a steady watch on Walesa outside Elektromontaz. A second car appeared the week of the ceremony, and it looked as if the authorities intended to arrest Walesa before the event. Workers developed a plan to smuggle Walesa out of Elektromontaz if the authorities came to arrest him. The day before the anniversary, a group of officials entered the company grounds and headed for the management offices. They had come for Walesa, and his colleagues bundled him into a car.

Walesa went to the Lenin Shipyard for the ceremony the next evening. He had promised the year before that more mourners would join them in 1979, and he was not disappointed. Climbing onto a wall in front of the shipyard, Walesa surveyed a crowd of 7,000 people and a semicircle of militia vehicles behind it. He described the events of the

I hadn't the slightest notion of how to manage a strike; I was out of my depth.
—LECH WALESA
on the 1970 strike

December strike as he had witnessed them and the responsibility he felt for the bloodshed that ended the strike. He told the crowd that Gierek had betrayed the people's trust and that solidarity was their only hope. "Only an organized and independent society can make itself heard. I beg you to organize yourselves in independent groups for your own self-defense," he said. The government had refused to build a monument in the workers' memory, and Walesa ended his speech with an appeal for the mourners to build the monument that the state denied them. "Next year on the tenth anniversary, each of you must bring a stone or brick to this spot. We shall cement them into place and we shall build a monument," he said.

Though Elektromontaz was shorthanded, the company announced soon after the ceremony that 14 workers, including Walesa and 12 other FTU members, were no longer needed. One of the fired workers, Jan Sczepanski, disappeared soon after his dismissal, and his dismembered body was later found in a canal. Sczepanski was only a teenager, but his murder clearly demonstrated that the authorities were willing to use brutal methods to break the opposition. As Walesa left his apartment the day of Sczepanski's funeral, he found himself surrounded by police, who grabbed a wreath he was carrying and threw him into a car.

Walesa was well known among active oppositionists in Gdansk before his speech at the memorial ceremony. Only after the speech and the scuffle with the police on the day of Sczepanski's funeral, however, did Walesa become known to ordinary Poles in Gdansk. His neighbors at the Stogi apartment complex, for example, thought of Walesa simply as the man who put religious pictures in his windows during holidays. Now his neighbors united in his support. On one occasion when the police came to arrest Walesa, his neighbors doused them with hot water, food, slippers, and other household items.

Unemployed again, Walesa could not support his family. He turned to Jacek Kuron, and KOR provided food and a lawyer to represent Walesa. The FTU continued to organize, and Walesa attended secret meetings throughout Gdansk and Gdynia.

> It is said that experience comes with age. Of course, but it also comes with action.
> —LECH WALESA

On July 1, 1980, the government announced new increases in meat prices. Strikes broke out across Poland. The Gierek government, having come to power after similar strikes toppled Gomulka, ordered managers to satisfy workers' demands quickly and quietly. Strike committees throughout Poland accepted the increases and promptly demanded higher increases than the ones they had just accepted. Government papers barely mentioned the strikes, hinting only at isolated "work stoppages." But Jacek Kuron spread the word, and workers throughout Poland learned they could easily extract wage increases from the nervous regime.

The most radical of the July strikes took place in Lublin, where railroad workers blocked the tracks between Poland and the Soviet Union. More important, though, the Lublin strikers did not limit their demands to economic issues. Their agenda included political demands — a five-day work week, an end to press censorship, and trade unions "that would not take orders from above." On August 9, Anna Walentynowicz was fired. After a meeting with Kuron the FTU decided the time was right for strike. The ambitious agenda of the Lublin strikers was, as one writer noted, merely a "dress rehearsal" for the main drama at the Lenin Shipyard.

Polish premier Piotr Jaroszewicz (slightly left of center), whom Walesa called "nothing but a Russian pawn," and Edward Gierek (waving, right of Jaroszewicz) appear at a May Day rally in 1979, Gierek's last year in power. Minister of National Defense Wojciech Jaruzelski (far left) looks on.

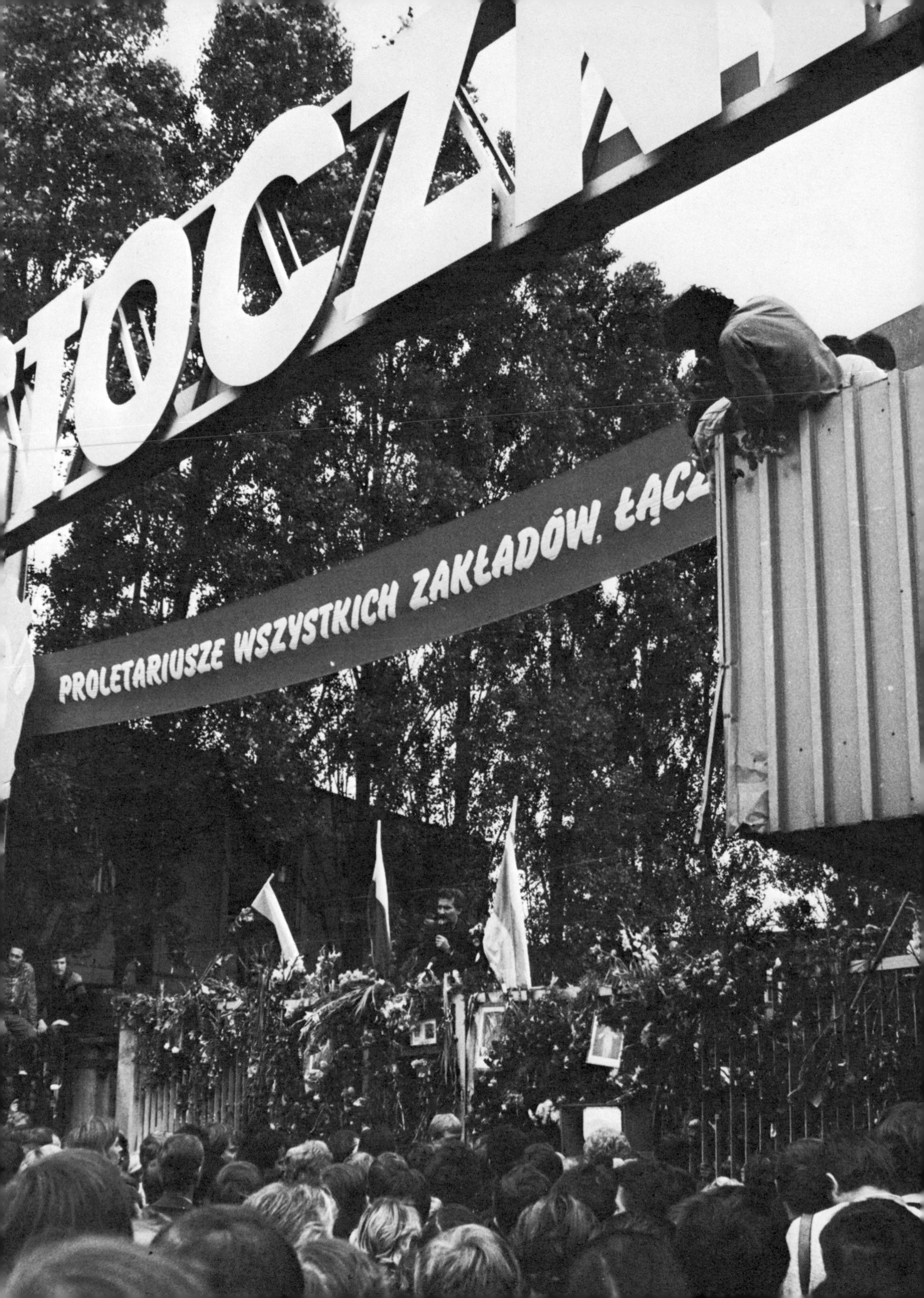

TOCZ
PROLETARIUSZE WSZYSTKICH ZAKŁADÓW, ŁĄCZ

4

The Shipyard Strikes

Climbing over the wall of the Lenin Shipyard on August 14, Walesa had no idea how the workers would greet a strike call. The FTU hoped Walentynowicz's dismissal would provide a catalyst, but the workers hesitated until Walesa's confrontation with the yard director, Klemens Gniech. Walesa jumped down from the bulldozer where he had shouted down Gniech, sent the director's limousine to pick up Walentynowicz, and formed a strike committee. Eager to avoid the violence that erupted when the workers took to the streets in 1970, Walesa insisted the strikers remain inside the shipyard gates.

The older workers who dominated the strike committee were more concerned with economic gains than political reforms; independent trade unions were never mentioned in the committee's initial demands. When the negotiations began in the meeting hall of the health and safety center, Gniech found himself facing Walesa, the strike committee, a crowd of 200 workers, and a list of demands that included the reinstatement of Walesa and Walentynowicz, a pay hike, no punishments for the strikers, and a monument to the workers killed in 1970.

Walesa emerged from the crowd as an authentic man, free, angry, decisive, behaving directly and speaking plainly.
—MARIA JANION
upon seeing Walesa for the first time

Before a crowd of workers at the Lenin Shipyard, Walesa foments a strike in August 1980. The workers made a list of 21 demands, including free speech, the right to strike, access to the news media, equal pay for equal work, and the release of all political prisoners.

Above the heads of striking workers at the Lenin Shipyard, a placard displays the Solidarity logo and the message 21 x TAK, which means 21 times yes. The 21 demands to which the placard refers included the right to establish trade unions that would function independently rather than under government supervision.

Gniech declared a monument out of the question. As for the other demands, Gniech would only discuss the wage increase, insisting that skilled workers receive larger raises. Walesa saw that Gniech was trying to divide the strikers, buying off one group at the expense of others. "We all want the same increase," Walesa insisted. "It's 2,000 for everybody or nothing." Eventually, Gniech agreed to the monument, which Walesa seized upon as a major concession. Grabbing a microphone, he told the workers they should continue the strike until all their demands were met.

The mood in the yard turned nervous and angry on August 15. The government had tried to isolate the strike by cutting off all phone lines to Gdansk, and Gniech refused to make any decision without appealing to "higher authority." If Gniech was just a government mouthpiece, the workers concluded, then party leaders in Warsaw should come to the shipyard and negotiate directly. The strike was losing momentum by Saturday, August 16. The strike committee voted to accept Gniech's offer to rehire Walentynowicz and Walesa and raise wages by 1,500 zlotys. Walesa reluctantly agreed. Gniech and Walesa announced the settlement, and workers began filing out of the yard.

The Lenin Shipyard was the largest enterprise in Gdansk, and workers from small factories throughout the city had come to the yard to support the strike, hoping the 20,000 shipyard workers would set a precedent for their own negotiations by taking a hard line with the authorities. Instead they found the shipyard had settled for a measly wage increase and had left them dangling out on a limb. As the strike broke up, a leader of the transport workers seized a microphone and denounced the shipyard strikers for betraying them. Other workers hacked apart loudspeakers with axes and scrawled "traitor" on the shipyard walls, referring to Walesa. Walesa found himself surrounded by thousands of angry workers. Realizing that he had badly misjudged the workers' mood, he decided to continue the strike.

Anna Walentynowicz had worked nearly 30 years at the Lenin Shipyard — 16 as a welder and 14 as a crane operator — when she was fired on August 7, 1980, for distributing political pamphlets. Her dismissal, just months before she was scheduled to retire, outraged Poland's working class and helped inspire her fellow workers to strike that month.

Walesa shouted through a bullhorn for the workers not to leave. Many of those departing ignored him, but others turned around and came back. A new strike committee was elected, and a new list of 21 demands was written.

The new committee replaced older, cautious workers with FTU leaders, including Walesa, Walentynowicz, Andrzej and Joanna Gwiazda, and Bogdan Lis. The committee's new demands reflected the ambitious program for political change that FTU leaders had developed in two years of opposition activity. Walesa later claimed he had planned all along to end the strike and begin it anew with a more radical leadership. In fact, he did not foresee the turn events would take after he announced the end of the strike. Yet his snap judgment to continue the strike set off a chain of events that transformed the strike into a national movement. "Solidarity was born at that precise moment when the shipyard strike evolved from a success in the shipyard to a strike in support of other factories and business enterprises, large and small, in need of our protection," Walesa later wrote.

The workers demanded independent trade unions, the right to strike, free speech, access to the media, and the release of all political prisoners. They called for an overhaul of the economy and demanded that economic managers be selected for their expertise rather than party loyalty. Only hours before, the strike had nearly ended with minor wage concessions for the shipyard workers. Now the stakes had been raised to a fight for sweeping political change waged on behalf of all Poles.

By Sunday, August 17, thousands of Poles had gathered at the Lenin Shipyard. Flowers, crucifixes, and photos of Pope John Paul II covered the gate. The workers handed copies of a strike bulletin through the fence to their supporters outside, who handed vats of soup, loaves of bread, and sacks of potatoes over the fence in return. Father Henryk Jankowski held a mass inside the yard and blessed a makeshift cross, which the workers cemented into place inside Gate No. 2 as a temporary monument to the workers killed in 1970. Father Jankowski gave Walesa a badge of the Black Madonna of Czes-

We shall conquer with unity.
—Polish shipyard workers

Families of striking workers surround the Lenin Shipyard in August 1980. In an effort to avoid the violence that had accompanied the strikes in Poland 10 years before, Walesa insisted that the strikers remain within the confines of the shipyard. Countless people surrounded the shipyard and adorned its gates with flowers and religious icons to show their support for the labor movement.

tochowa, the holiest shrine in Poland. Walesa wore the badge throughout the strike, and Jankowski became a principal adviser to Walesa.

Walesa established a remarkable rapport with the workers. Each night, they pushed him up onto the fence at Gate No. 2 to deliver his "evening vespers." Describing the day's events and debates within the leadership, Walesa spoke briefly and concisely, illustrating his points with gestures and ironic jokes. His plainspoken and spontaneous manner were the opposite of the dogmatic voice of Polish communism. The authorities spoke in a dull, plodding prose, whereas Walesa spoke quickly and naturally. The government issued commands, whereas Walesa told the strikers, "I am not your master, I am your servant."

To strengthen their resolve, striking workers pray and consult with clergymen at the Lenin Shipyard in August 1980. That month, Walesa emerged as head of the Inter-Factory Strike Committee (MKS), empowered to negotiate with the government on behalf of all Polish workers.

Walesa spoke to thousands of workers as if they were a single person, making the workers feel as though he were speaking to each one of them individually. Even he was surprised by his hold over the workers. "For the first time, my words were entirely in step with my thoughts, and with the plan that I was trying to communicate with my audience." Walesa was coming into his own during those speeches, and he became convinced that only he could bring the strikes to a successful conclusion. He later wrote, "I really felt, however arrogant it might sound, that if anything was to be achieved, it was up to me to achieve it." Walesa, of course, was only one member of a collective leadership, and his autocratic style would alienate many members of the strike committee in the coming days.

Still, the same stubborn belief in his own leadership that led Walesa to push aside his colleagues also lent an infectious confidence to his every word and gesture. On the rostrum in front of Gate No. 2, he thrust his fists into the air and spread his fingers into a *V* for victory, as if the strike's ultimate triumph were inevitable. During tense moments he often broke out into the national anthem. When Walesa sang the line "Poland shall not perish so long as we live," he reminded the strikers that they had to remain united at any cost.

In late August, Walesa asked a group of leading academics to organize a small team of advisers to help the strike committee negotiate with the government. However, several strike committee members objected to the advisers. Walesa seemed too willing to compromise, and they feared the advisers would only try to soften the committee's proposals even more. Walesa, however, argued that the advisers would provide a much-needed moderating influence on the strike committee.

Walesa's support for the advisers also reinforced the national character of the shipyard strike. Over 250 factories had gone on strike all over Poland, and they had agreed to form an Inter-Factory Strike Committee (MKS) at the Lenin Shipyard to coordinate their demands. Walesa and his colleagues were now negotiating for all Polish workers, indeed, for all of Polish society. In his support for the expert advisers and his relationship with Father Jankowski, Walesa had brought the church and the intellectuals into the strike leadership, uniting the opposition forces that had begun to come together after 1976.

Walesa offered to step down from the MKS on the eve of the negotiations. He still felt responsible for the workers killed in 1970. He worried that the longer the strikes continued, the more likely they, too, would end in bloodshed. He feared his past conflicts with the authorities might hinder a quick agreement, but the MKS rejected his resignation. The government delegation, led by Deputy Prime Minister Mieczyslaw Jagielski, arrived on August 23. The workers surrounded the negotiators as they entered the gates in a limousine, demanding they get out and walk. "On your knees!" the workers shouted. Walesa asked the workers to calm themselves and let the delegation pass.

Jagielski wanted to meet privately with Walesa and the MKS presidium, but the strikers had no intention of holding secret talks. Walesa led Jagielski into a shipyard conference hall. Workers jeered at the government team from behind a plate of glass. The negotiators faced off on opposite sides of a Formica coffee table. Their every word was piped over loudspeakers for the 10,000 strikers to hear.

He wanted to be merely a trade unionist, but the situation in Poland forced him to act in a way which his adversaries always defined as political.
—ANDRZEJ DRZYCIMSKI
journalist

Walesa escorts Deputy Prime Minister Mieczyslaw Jagielski, leader of the government delegation appointed to negotiate with the workers. Though certain that the government would not act in good faith, the workers hoped that Walesa would be able to get the government to agree to at least some of their 21 demands.

Walesa put Jagielski on the defensive immediately, berating him about show trials and the recent arrest of three KOR activists. Jagielski claimed Poland had no political prisoners and that show trials had never occurred. Walesa refused to play along. "Prime Minister, these three cases are known to us and to the public. We know what kind of trials they were. . . . I can say straight out because I'm a worker and don't mince words, that they were fixed." The strikers' roaring cheers reverberated inside the conference hall. Though Jagielski rejected nearly all the strikers' demands, Walesa, by standing up to the government, had given his fellow workers a new sense of their own strength.

During the next few days, workers in overalls and black berets gathered under loudspeakers to listen to the negotiations, which were making little progress. Workers inside the conference hall slept on blankets and air mattresses. MKS delegates representing strikers all over the country talked and waited for news. The strikers passed the time writing poetry or making confessions to Father Jankowski. During breaks in the negotiations, Walesa raced through the conference hall signing autographs or sat with one of his children on his knee as he spoke with delegates. Every couple of days, Walesa spoke with Danuta at the shipyard gates. Seeing Walesa banter with the workers and watching his remarkable influence over them, Danuta realized the strike had changed their lives. "I knew Lech was drawing away from me," she later said. "He was with all those people, and I realized life was going to be different from then on."

Jagielski was steadfast in his opposition to independent unions. On Monday, August 25, the advisers asked the MKS presidium whether they would accept a compromise, perhaps reformed government trade unions. The presidium refused. "If I gave in on this," Walesa said, "I would be swept away." On Tuesday and Wednesday, Andrzej Gwiazda, Lis, and the advisers met privately with Jagielski's negotiating team. For 35 years, Polish Communists had ruled Poland in the name of the working class. The demand for independent trade unions denied the government's claim to be the workers' sole representative. This, the government team argued, neither Moscow nor Warsaw could accept. The negotiators said the authorities could, hypothetically, agree to new trade unions that explicitly accepted "the leading role of the party." The advisers responded that the new unions would not be independent if the party controlled them. Instead, the strikers could acknowledge the party's leading role "in the state." Thus, the unions would remain independent of the government while recognizing the Communists' right to govern the nation.

The MKS presidium wanted to put the agreement to a vote by the strikers. The leadership had taken great pains to act democratically, and now the key issue, independent unions, was being negotiated behind closed doors. Walesa defended this as merely "a tactical maneuver." He believed a divisive debate over accepting the party's leading role would only weaken the strike. No agreement would be signed without approval from the full MKS, he promised. Walesa's assurances failed to quell the discussion. As tempers rose and heated words passed between the delegates, Walesa broke out into the national anthem, and the delegates stopped their arguments to join him.

Workers listen to a speech at a Lenin Shipyard meeting hall. Despite Jagielski's request that they be private, the discussions between Solidarity leaders and the government were transmitted over loudspeakers located in shipyard buildings such as this one so that workers and their supporters could follow the progress of the debate.

Striking workers await the fate of their 21 demands. The painted wooden sign reads, JUSTICE AND EQUALITY FOR THE WHOLE NATION; the message on the wall reads, ONLY SOLIDARITY.

Unbeknownst to the strikers, the main sticking point had been resolved. On Thursday, August 28, Jagielski seemed close to accepting the right to strike and a free press. An agreement seemed near, but Jagielski never arrived for negotiations on Friday. Rumors ripped through the Lenin Shipyard that the government was preparing to turn the army loose on the strikers.

Jagielski returned on Saturday, August 30, in a festive mood, evidently having cleared the remaining issues with party leaders in Warsaw. Jagielski initialed the first point of the agreement, pledging

the government to permit independent trade unions that acknowledged that "the PZPR plays the leading role in the state." Under the second point, the government would give immunity to the strikers and their "supporters," referring to KOR activists like Jacek Kuron and Adam Michnik, who had been arrested during the strike. Jagielski tried to divide the strikers from the intellectuals, holding out the prospect of an agreement if only the strikers would let the government resolve the matter of what to do with these "insignificant supporters." When Jagielski tried to change the subject, Walesa said there might be another strike if the government did not free the KOR activists. Jagielski agreed to discuss the matter with party leaders in Warsaw and return the next day.

It seemed as though an agreement would finally be signed. Inside the conference hall, however, the MKS delegates were in an uproar. Walesa's statement that there would be another strike if the KOR activists were not released suggested that he was willing to end the current strike with the KOR activists still behind bars. To most of the delegates, Walesa was betraying the workers' KOR allies in his hurry to strike a bargain. As delegates denounced the agreements, Walesa repeatedly leaped to the microphone and cut off speakers in mid-sentence. By the end of the discussion, Walesa had received cheers of approval for three different and contradictory positions on the KOR prisoners.

Walesa stuck to his original position, telling Jagielski there would be another strike if the KOR activists were not released. However, Walesa's flurry of proposals struck many delegates as manipulative. They felt he was being high-handed when he cut off speakers with whom he disagreed. These delegates saw his behavior as an affront to the democratic spirit of the strike. To a growing number of Walesa's critics, he seemed less concerned with the substance of the arguments than with silencing the arguments altogether. But Walesa believed the strikers could not afford to reopen negotiations. Gierek could fall any day, and then the strikers would have to start over with new and probably more stubborn

> *I see Walesa as a man of instinct, not intellect. He is in my opinion, a man of considerable innate intelligence that he has never tried to develop or refine.*
> —LECH BADKOWSKI
> Solidarity columnist

negotiating partners. As long as the workers had independent unions, Walesa believed the rest of their hopes would be realized.

The strikers had heard the acrimonious dispute over the loudspeaker, and a confused silence fell over the yard. When Walesa mounted a bulldozer in front of Gate No. 2, he seemed to have left the bitter debates far behind. Blinded by the glare of electric lights, Walesa was calm and relaxed. His speech sounded more like a chat with a friend than a speech to thousands of workers. "And now," he concluded, "we'll all go to our homes, take a bath, go to bed and tomorrow, later, our Poland will have more citizens. And now, therefore, let us sing the national anthem for this country of ours. Oh, and one more thing," he added. "Let us sing a religious song to God because now we can't go any further without God." The workers carried Walesa through the yard, singing, "May he live a hundred years."

By midafternoon the next day, each point was initialed, and the agreement was presented to the MKS presidium. Walesa began to read a speech, but put it down. "Beloved friends," he said, "You have trusted me so far, so I beg you to trust me now. We have got all we could in the present situation. The rest we will get in time, because we now have the most important thing of all . . . our independent, self-governing trade unions. That is our guarantee for the future."

Then the MKS presidium and the government team marched into the conference hall to sign the agreements before the MKS delegates and the television cameras that captured the scene and relayed it throughout Poland and around the world. Walesa offered his thanks and congratulations to the delegates and strikers. "We have fought, not for ourselves nor for our own interests," he told them, "but for the entire country. We have fought for all of you. And now, with the same determination and solidarity that we showed on strike, we shall go back to work. As of tomorrow, the new life of our trade union begins. Let's take care that it remains independent and self-governing, working for us all and for the good of the country, for Poland. I proclaim that the strike is over."

Walesa led the MKS delegates in the national anthem one final time and commended the government negotiators for resolving the strike by "talking as Poles talk to Poles." With that, the texts of the agreement were spread out on a table. On the wall over the agreements hung a cross, a Polish flag, and a bust of Lenin, the founder of the Soviet state. Jagielski put his signature to the agreements, and then Walesa signed with an enormous pen topped by a tassel and a picture of Pope John Paul II.

Walesa ended the strike where he had begun it — in the shipyard talking to the workers. He told them that the government radio would broadcast mass from that day forward and that the KOR activists would soon be released. Walesa's talks with the workers had fortified him throughout the strike, and he wanted them to leave with some understanding of why he had not always acted as democratically as his opponents would have liked. "Even if I sound like a dictator, I have always felt responsible for the blood that was shed in December 1970. It was partly due to my own incompetent leadership. So I want us to meet here on every December 16 at this place. I shall be here, even if I have to crawl on hands and knees. Remember that. And I shall always tell you the truth in this holy place."

A triumphant Lech Walesa is carried on the shoulders of two of his fellow workers. On August 29, after 15 days of negotiations, the Polish government granted the workers the right to form independent trade unions, the most significant step for Polish labor in 35 years.

5
Solidarity

Poland's new union set up quarters in Gdansk's seedy Hotel Morski. The union called itself Solidarity, after the title of the strikers' daily bulletin and the unity that had animated the strike. Walesa became chairman of Solidarity's Temporary National Committee. He converted a corner bedroom into an office, sparsely furnished with a desk and the cross that had hung in the shipyard conference hall.

Walesa had hoped to work part-time at the shipyard, but the strike had transformed him from an unemployed electrician into a full-time union leader. Journalists beamed his comments over news wires around the world. Politicians invited Walesa to France, the United States, and Japan, hoping to share in a small piece of his prestige. Delegations from across Poland flocked to Gdansk for advice on how to establish Solidarity branches, and just about all of them wanted to meet with Walesa.

> *SOLIDARITY was born at that precise moment when the shipyard strike evolved from a local success in the shipyard to a strike in support of other factories . . . large and small, in need of our protection.*
> —LECH WALESA
> on the advent of Solidarity

Walesa and Andrzej Gwiazda visit a mine in Walbrzych, Poland, in December 1980. By this time Walesa had become a full-time union leader and Gwiazda had climbed through Solidarity's ranks to become the union's number-two man.

Walesa enjoyed the attention. Still, he had spent his entire life working with his hands. Now he was strapped to a desk. Solidarity was a movement of workers and ordinary Poles, and Walesa believed he could only spread the national unity the strike had achieved by speaking to them as often as possible. Solidarity represented basic moral values as well as a political and economic program. Poles saw Walesa as the embodiment of those values, and he tried to show that he still shared them.

The divisions between Walesa and other strike leaders that had emerged at the Lenin Shipyard surfaced quickly in the union's National Committee. Some thought all the adulation had gone to Walesa's head. The government gave him a new six-room apartment in a fashionable Gdansk district soon after the strike. He and Danuta now had six children, and the family had long ago outgrown its small apartment at Stogi. Walesa had applied for a new apartment long before the strike, and he felt entitled to it. But many people objected that Walesa was allowing the government to win him over with special treatment. Walesa also seemed to have little patience for the democratic process within the union.

The Walesa family in September 1980 (left to right): Lech, Magdalena, Danuta, Anna (on her mother's lap), Bogdan, Przemyslaw, Jaroslaw (displaying a drawing), and Slavomir.

He took to wearing a coat and tie at Solidarity meetings and often arrived late. When he finally did show up, he often fell asleep or made faces for photographers.

The National Committee also disagreed about how quickly Solidarity should push for change. The government had agreed to sweeping reforms, but they remained to be enacted. Walesa thought Solidarity should try to cooperate with the government as the agreements were implemented. Other union leaders saw Walesa surrounding himself with moderate advisers — church officials and the experts he had brought into the strike leadership. The FTU group feared Walesa was too eager to compromise. Shortly after the strike, Anna Walentynowicz visited Walesa in his new appartment and suggested that he resign in favor of a more radical leader, perhaps Andrzej Gwiazda or Jacek Kuron.

Walesa refused to step down. He saw his rapport with the workers as the source of his authority, and both Walesa and his opponents knew he still had the workers' support, which was all the endorsement Walesa felt he needed. Nonetheless, as the government reneged on various provisions of the agreement, Walesa's disagreements with his colleagues continued to grow.

Solidarity had thrown the Communist party into disarray. Stanislaw Kania replaced Edward Gierek

Walesa and Gwiazda negotiate with leaders of the Polish government at the Council of Ministers building in Warsaw in October 1980. Though the government had agreed to permit independent trade unions, its "leading role" remained a point of debate. Solidarity leaders made it clear that strikes would ensue if that role was anything more than peripheral.

only days after the Gdansk agreements were signed. The party tried to reassert authority by provoking confrontations with Solidarity. On October 24, Walesa led a stream of happy followers into a Warsaw courthouse to register the union. The crowd cheered as the judge accepted the union's statutes. He added, however, that the statutes required certain amendments, including a statement that the union accepted the party's "leading role" and Poland's alliance with the Soviet Union. Walesa and the Solidarity activists were shocked.

Walesa was furious at the judge's decision, because it would allow the government to determine what actions violated the party's leading role. The authorities could disband the union for violating its own statutes. Still, Walesa and his advisers advocated a moderate response, an appeal to the supreme court. Regional Solidarity leaders agreed with Walesa, but a majority of the National Committee wanted to declare a general strike. Calls from local Solidarity offices around the country made clear the rank and file was ready for a showdown. An appeal was filed with the highest court of law, and the National Committee announced that a nationwide strike would begin if the court did not register Solidarity by November 12. Walesa still hoped to secure Solidarity's registration through negotiations, but a meeting with Jagielski produced no agreement.

Solidarity activists distributed detailed strike plans all over Poland, but the strike was called off when the court issued a compromise on November 10. The tension that had built up the week before the court's ruling was released in victory celebrations. Walesa was the guest of honor at a festival of poetry and song at the Warsaw Opera House. A Solidarity logo in wavy red letters hung over the stage. A banner addressed to Walesa read, DON'T BE AFRAID; THE NATION IS WITH YOU.

The celebration was brief for Walesa. On November 20, the police arrested Jan Narozniak, a young mathematician and union activist who had obtained a government document outlining a plan to eliminate "illegal antisocialist activity." Zbigniew Bujak, Solidarity's Warsaw chairman, demanded Narozniak's immediate release and a public inves-

He behaves and talks as someone charged, electrified by the collective body.
—MARIA JANION

tigation of the security police. Bujak threatened to call a general strike in Warsaw on November 27 if the government refused to negotiate these demands.

To Walesa, this was a just cause that needed to be settled by other means. The Gdansk agreements had never mentioned curbs on the security police, and Solidarity was rapidly losing control of its members. Strikes began breaking out before Bujak's deadline. The U.S. State Department issued an ominous warning about Soviet troop movements on the Polish border. Narozniak was released at dawn on the 27th, but strikes continued to spread. The government flew Walesa to Warsaw, and he, Bujak, and Kuron tried to contain the strikes, but the workers only returned to work after the government agreed to talks on the police.

Walesa called for an end to further strikes. The wildcat strikes showed that Solidarity could not control its members, and they raised fears in the Soviet Union that the party was losing control over the country. Walesa feared the next crisis could end with a Soviet invasion, and the church was pressuring him to make sure the union did not endanger Poland's independence. In appealing to workers to stay on the job, Walesa was calling for a truce between the government and society.

The idea of a monument to the workers killed in 1970 had obsessed Walesa for a decade. At the ceremony on December 16, 1979, he had promised the mourners that they would build a monument the following year. On December 16, 1980, he showed them the results of their handiwork. The ceremony began at 5:00 P.M. under falling sleet. A Polish actor read out a roll call of the fallen workers. After each name, the crowd of 150,000 people declared solemnly, "He is still with us."

As Walesa stood at the base of the monument, he saw before him Solidarity leaders, Catholic bishops, party officials, and military officers standing side by side — a symbol of the national unity he was calling for. Over Walesa's head towered three steel crosses hung with anchors, symbolizing the crushed rebellions of 1956, 1970, and 1976. The anchor was the Polish national symbol during World

Lech Walesa onstage at the Warsaw Opera House in November 1980. Workers celebrated the supreme court's decision to validate the Solidarity charter with a festival of poetry and music at the opera house, and Walesa was the guest of honor.

War II, and the monument charged the authorities with a heinous crime, the crucifixion of Poland.

The monument's message was bitter indeed. To see it finally built was a measure of how far Poland had come since August. It was a personal triumph for Walesa, but he used the occasion to remind Poles of the need for restraint. Walesa had never read a prepared speech before. In August he had always found the right words to convey his feelings spontaneously. Now he felt trapped by a written text, and he read it awkwardly. He could barely see his audience through the glare of the floodlights as he commanded them to "keep peace and order, and to respect all laws and authorities . . . to show prudence and reflection in all actions for the good of the fatherland."

By 1981 the economy had further deteriorated, and the partnership promised in the Gdansk agreements had yet to take shape. To the government, partnership meant that Solidarity should use its influence with the workers to prevent strikes and accept unpopular policies to right the economy. Solidarity recognized the need to take action on the economy, but it refused to accept responsibility for government policies unless workers had more control over managing the economy, a direct challenge to the party's "leading role." The two sides were headed for a collision, and Walesa was standing right in the middle of it.

In January, Walesa returned from a visit with Pope John Paul II in Rome. He was greeted by Poles bearing flowers and reports about new crises over the five-day workweek and the registration of a new farmers' union, Rural Solidarity. The Gdansk agreements had made Saturday a day of rest, but the government declared that Poles would only have two free Saturdays a month. The decision went to the heart of the partnership issue, demonstrating that the government had no intention of consulting Solidarity on basic trade union issues. Strikes broke out, and Walesa left for a round of travels to try to contain the strikes.

Speaking to farmers in Rzeszow, Walesa declared that if the government opened up its books, "and we reckon the position's really bad, we will go to work on Sunday! Even if the priests shout at us!" Walesa's statement surprised the farmers, but it represented a consensus within Solidarity that Poles should be willing to work on Saturdays if the government could prove it was economically necessary. The National Committee announced a nationwide general strike for February 3 if the government did not resolve the issues of free Saturdays and freedom of information. Walesa led a negotiating team to begin talks with Prime Minister Jozef Pinkowski on January 30. The talks went on until well after midnight. The two sides made no progress on Rural Solidarity, but they agreed that Poles would work only one Saturday a month and that Solidarity could publish a weekly magazine. The state radio and television would also report statements by Solidarity's National Committee.

On February 9, General Wojciech Jaruzelski replaced Stanislaw Kania as prime minister. Because Jaruzelski was a general, Poles considered him a nationalist. He had been deported to a labor camp in the Soviet Union in 1939 and had reportedly refused to turn the army loose on the strikes at the Lenin Shipyard. Jaruzelski's stiff manner intrigued Walesa, and he wondered what lay behind the dark glasses Jaruzelski always wore. During their first meeting, Jaruzelski commended Walesa on his military record, which the general seemed to have studied in detail. Walesa was impressed by Jaruzelski's lively way of speaking, a pleasant contrast to the dogmatic lectures Kania had subjected him to. Walesa felt he had established an understanding with Jaruzelski that he hoped would begin a process of compromise between Solidarity and the government.

Solidarity agreed to a 90-day moratorium on strikes that was suggested by Jaruzelski. But the issue of Rural Solidarity remained unresolved. On March 14, Walesa traveled to Radom and asked Solidarity leaders there to end a wildcat strike. That same day, Jan Rulewski, a Rural Solidarity leader, began a sit-in at a government building in Bydgoszcz, demanding that the authorities certify the union. On March 19, 200 police expelled the demonstrators, beating them with truncheons.

More than 150,000 Poles gather at the front gate of the Lenin Shipyard on December 16, 1980, to honor the workers who were killed in the labor riots of 1970. At the ceremony, leaders of the Roman Catholic church, the Communist party, and Solidarity called for a reconciliation for the sake of Poland's future.

Pope John Paul II greets Lech and Danuta Walesa in Rome on January 15, 1981. The Pope told the Walesas, "I believe the cornerstone of your venture, which began in August 1980 in the coastal region and in other great centers of Polish industry, was a common impulse to promote the moral good of society."

The National Committee met on March 23. To most members the question was not whether, but when, to call a general strike. Walesa believed a strike would only invite a civil war. He wanted the National Committee to call a brief warning strike instead. If the government did not punish those responsible for the Bydgoszcz attack, a general strike would follow. The heated debate continued all night. At 3:00 A.M., Walesa stood up and gave his colleagues an ultimatum. They had eight hours to adopt his position. If they refused, he would resign. Walesa's resignation would split the union, which Solidarity could ill afford. The National Committee adopted Walesa's position, but his autocratic manner and his refusal to submit to majority rule poisoned relations with his colleagues.

Solidarity had nearly 10 million members now, 80 percent of all Polish workers. The country prepared for a strike as if it were going to war. Buildings were draped in red-and-white flags, the union's official colors. Workers wearing Solidarity badges and armbands guarded factories. On March 27, sirens signaled workers around the country to lay down their tools. Walesa toured Warsaw, urging support for the Jaruzelski government. "This is a uniform we can trust," he said. At noon, Poles ended their impressive show of force and returned to work.

As the country prepared for the main event, the church and Walesa's advisers pressured him to avoid a general strike. Walesa opened discussions with Deputy Prime Minister Mieczyslaw Rakowski, who was widely regarded as an advocate of reform. In the past, a negotiating team had always accompanied Walesa in talks with the government. This time, however, Walesa told other Solidarity leaders he alone would meet with Rakowski. The situation was grave, he said, and "democracy must be limited."

Walesa told Rakowski that Polish workers could no longer tolerate police violence after the bloodshed of 1956, 1970, and 1976. "We cannot allow the militia to beat us up," he said. Rakowski refused to certify Rural Solidarity, offering instead to turn the matter over to the Polish parliament and to make sure that those responsible for the Bydgoszcz incident were prosecuted. Rakowski provided no guarantees that the parliament would register Rural Solidarity, but Walesa wanted to avoid a general strike, which he considered a break with Solidarity's program for evolutionary change. Soviet troops were conducting maneuvers in Poland and might respond to a general strike with force, and Solidarity would be crushed. As long as Solidarity continued to exist, however, Walesa believed it could still achieve its goals. Walesa accepted the "Warsaw Agreement."

Walesa knew the agreement would not be popular, so instead of presenting it to the full National Committee he submitted it to a small group of members empowered to act on the committee's behalf in emergency situations. The agreement was approved, the general strike suspended. Walesa had avoided a confrontation with the government, but the Warsaw Agreement only exacerbated tensions within Solidarity. The National Committee met the next day in the conference hall at the Lenin Shipyard, where Walesa had faced angry opponents in August. Workers grumbled that Walesa and his advisers were too frightened about a Soviet invasion. The committee approved the decision to suspend the strike but at-

General Wojciech Jaruzelski salutes at a May Day celebration in Warsaw in 1983. Jaruzelski replaced Stanislaw Kania as Poland's prime minister in 1981 during a period of intense and widespread labor unrest. One week after Jaruzelski's inauguration, the workers called off all strikes as a gesture of goodwill toward the new leader.

tacked Walesa for the way the strike had been canceled. Andrzej Gwiazda and Solidarity spokesman Karol Modzelewski denounced him for undermining democracy within the union. "The king and his men" had too much power, Modzelewski said, and he for one could no longer serve them.

Walesa was the unrivaled leader of Solidarity, but a majority of the union disagreed with his moderate course, and he now saw himself as standing between the extreme positions of the union and the government. He believed Solidarity was walking into a confrontation with the government, and it was his responsibility to prevent a showdown between them. "I won't allow things to come to a confrontation," he told the National Committee. "The point is not to smash your head open in one day, but to win, step by step . . . and as long as I'm here, that's how we're going to walk, step by step and cautiously."

Farm workers demonstrate in the Bydgoszcz province in February 1981, demanding government approval of the Free Farmers Union. Authorities broke up the demonstration with clubs and tear gas.

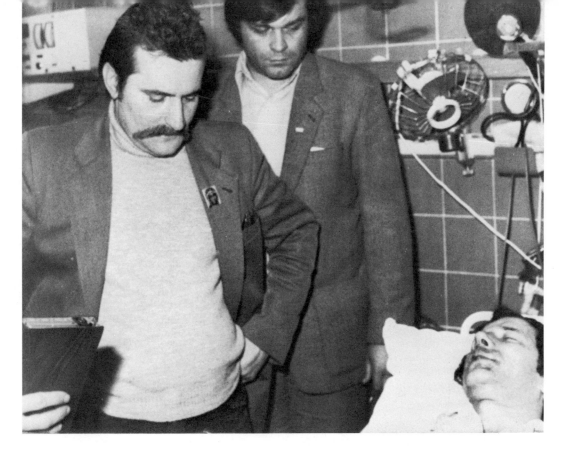

Walesa's stubborn nature contributed to the growing rift in the National Committee that reflected a basic tension in Solidarity's program. On the one hand, Solidarity claimed it did not want political power. On the other hand, it was founded to create a degree of democracy within a country ruled by an authoritarian regime. To foster democracy in Poland, Walesa's critics argued, Solidarity had to conduct its own affairs democratically. Thus, Walesa violated a fundamental principle when he took matters into his own hands. When the government refused to live up to the agreements, it forced Solidarity to take increasingly radical measures, and Solidarity only became more of a threat to the government. Until the Bydgoszcz incident, Solidarity had always accepted the position of Walesa and the moderates to preserve unity. From March onward, however, Solidarity increasingly followed the course of the radical majority. Walesa's differences with his colleagues grew, and the confrontation he sought to avoid drew closer.

Though most workers initially thought Jaruzelski would bring a new spirit of cooperation to Polish labor relations, his government soon authorized the violent repression of union activists. Here, Walesa visits Jan Rulewski, a regional Solidarity president, who was hospitalized after being beaten by police at a demonstration in Bydgoszcz, Poland.

6

Confrontation

An undeclared truce presided over Poland in the spring of 1981. Both Solidarity and the Polish Communist party turned inward as they prepared for separate national congresses. Strikes subsided in April, and *Solidarity Weekly*, provided for in Walesa's Warsaw Agreement with Rakowski, began to appear. In May, Solidarity received airtime on the state radio and television, and Rural Solidarity was registered.

Walesa traveled to Japan during this respite. Walesa captivated the Japanese, even as he criticized unionists for being too loyal to management and took a scissors to the tie of a union leader at an official reception. Walesa's ability to identify with his audience was the key to his ability to communicate. Though he spoke not a word of Japanese, he reached out across a tremendous cultural divide to establish a bond with his hosts.

His strength comes from understanding people, in the most elementary situations, but also in the entire span of experience.
—MARIA JANION

Workers take part in a Solidarity demonstration on the streets of Krakow, Poland, in June 1981. Antigovernment protests such as this one erupted throughout Poland that spring, as the country's industrial and agricultural production dropped steadily and Solidarity demands remained unmet.

Walesa speaks before an audience of Japanese workers in Tokyo on May 11, 1981. The Japanese saw Walesa as a kind of Polish samurai warrior, struggling against nearly impossible odds to defend not only his own honor but also that of his people.

The party's Extraordinary Congress in July only tightened the stalemate between hard-liners who wanted to crack down on Solidarity and reformists who wanted to compromise with it. The party's paralysis meant Solidarity could no longer promise its members that forgoing strikes would lead to economic change.

Solidarity had to offer some program to its increasingly impatient members. The economy had taken another downward spiral by the summer, and the government began to ration meat and other staple foods. Lines lengthened, and Poles grew more frustrated with the daily battle they waged to secure their most basic needs. Hunger strikes took place all over Poland.

Solidarity issued a proposal for factory self-government. Workers would elect representatives to decide how to run their enterprises and distribute profits. The proposal directly threatened the nomenklatura, the system of rewarding party members with plum jobs as economic managers. Solidarity had asked for information about the economy. Now it was asking for direct control over it. The government denounced Solidarity's plans as further proof that the union sought political power.

Walesa led a Solidarity negotiating team for talks with Rakowski on self-government in August, but the talks quickly broke down. When Walesa presented the union's plan, Rakowski responded with a list of the government's demands, including support for government price increases and an end to political activity. Essentially, the government was asking Solidarity to act as an official trade union and to use its influence to gain support for the government's unpopular economic program.

Solidarity responded with even bolder demands, calling for democratic elections to the Polish parliament. The union also created a Social Control Commission to supervise the production and distribution of food. Walesa believed Poles had to make some sacrifices to improve the economy, and Solidarity asked members to work eight Saturdays in the next year. The workers would themselves distribute whatever they produced on these days. Walesa saw the plan as an alternative to strikes.

"Instead of stopping work when we strike, which only drives the country to ruin," Walesa said, "we should strike by increasing productivity, and then requisitioning the goods we produce for our own needs." The government had asked the union to help bring the economy out of its decline. It remained to be seen whether the government would surrender a degree of its power in return. At a press conference inaugurating the program, Walesa declared that "we find ourselves at a crossroads."

Solidarity remained in a deadlock with the authorities as it prepared to hold its first National Congress in September. Both sides had enough power to reject the other's decisions, but neither had enough power to carry through a program. Walesa believed Poles were looking to the congress to find a way out of this impasse. The congress needed to decide "if and how we could reach a compromise with the government that would make it possible to fit Solidarity into the Polish political scene as an independent force and one not subordinate to the party."

Opening the congress at the Oliwa sports stadium in Gdansk, Walesa welcomed government observers politely and then paused. "I am not a diplomat, so I will be frank," Walesa said. "We are expected to answer various questions. We shall debate them.

Hunger marchers demonstrate in Krakow on August 7, 1981. That summer, Poland's economy was at a serious low: Food shortages emptied shelves and closed shops, lines grew longer, the government began rationing meat, angry Poles organized protest marches, and much of the country's labor force walked off the job.

Warsaw transit workers strike in August 1981. The city ground to a halt when thousands of bus and railroad workers organized a strike, making numerous demands similar to those being made by Solidarity. The strike dealt a harsh blow to the already faltering Polish economy.

But it is also we who are expecting an answer to the basic question. A year ago, we said that we are talking 'like a Pole to a Pole.' Now, twelve months of many conflicts later, we want to know whether we shall continue to talk like that." The phrase "like a Pole to a Pole" had become a catchword for a new spirit of cooperation and national unity ever since Walesa first uttered it at the end of the negotiations at the Lenin Shipyard in August. Walesa was asking the authorities whether they still intended to conduct themselves like Poles, whether they remained part of the Polish nation. Solidarity delegates cheered wildly.

A government law on factory self-management that ignored all Solidarity's proposals was nearing adoption in the Polish parliament. At the end of the first session of the Solidarity congress, the delegates issued an ultimatum, demanding that the parliament reject the government's law and enact Solidarity's proposal. If the government refused to do so, Solidarity would hold a public referendum to decide the matter. The delegates also issued a "Message to the Workers of Eastern Europe," inviting them "to join the workers' struggle." The prospect that strikes and demands for independent unions would spread like an infection to the rest of the Soviet bloc had become the worst nightmare of Soviet officialdom. Now, Solidarity was openly trying to spread what Soviet leaders called "the Polish disease." The Polish government attacked the message viciously, and Poles realized that the final showdown with the government was near.

Walesa viewed the self-management ultimatum as unrealistic, the message to Eastern European workers as senselessly provocative. He wanted the congress to work on a program to cooperate with the authorities to right the economy. Instead, Walesa believed, the congress had provoked a new confrontation with "rowdy stage effects." With the congress in recess for two weeks, Walesa met with Rakowski to reach a compromise on factory self-government. He submitted the deal to the Solidarity presidium rather than the full National Committee, and it was approved three to one.

The Polish parliament adopted the compromise quickly, and the sense of impending doom subsided. But the agreement allowed the government to veto Solidarity nominations for factory managers. Many Solidarity activists believed Walesa had settled for less than he should have. Walesa's opponents still avoided openly criticizing his policy of moderation and compromise, preferring instead to question his undemocratic methods. When the congress reconvened in late September, it debated the compromise, focusing on how Walesa had arrived at the deal and gotten approval for it. Why, delegates asked, had Walesa only consulted with a handful of expert advisers before accepting the offer? What had happened to the congress's ultimatum about a national referendum? And precisely why had he not waited for a full meeting of the National Committee to approve the deal?

Walesa defended himself forcefully. It was not his fault only four members of the presidium had come to the meeting, he said. Walesa had managed to get there even though he was sick at the time. If the delegates wanted to know why the meeting was sparsely attended, they should ask those who had failed to appear. The delegates adopted a motion that reprimanded Walesa for not submitting the proposal to the full National Committee and that praised Jan Rulewski, the Rural Solidarity leader injured in the Bydgoszcz incident, for voting against Walesa's compromise.

Walesa's action had dispelled the crisis, but his heavy-handed methods hung over the congress's election of a new chairman to the National Committee. Before the vote, the candidates — Walesa, Andrzej Gwiazda, and Jan Rulewski — made two speeches followed by a round of questions. In the first round of speeches, Walesa received a chilly welcome compared to the loud applause for Gwiazda and Rulewski. Tense and nervous, Walesa spoke stiffly. His call for unity in a second speech struck a chord in the delegates, however. "Let us leave our arguments, let us stay together, victory is possible for us." It was already midnight by the time Walesa's turn came to question the other candidates. Walesa

> *He never used invective or insults. It has to be put down to his refinement, not forgetting his close ties with the Christian ethic.*
> —BOLESLAW FAC
> Polish writer

said he was "tired of questions" and that he had none. Raising his fists, he suggested jokingly that the candidates settle their differences the old-fashioned way. "Anyone got a pair of boxing gloves?" he asked.

Walesa won the election, but with only 55 percent of the vote. Six months before, the delegates would not have even bothered counting the ballots. The delegates had come to resent the autocratic methods Walesa used to restrain the union's radical actions. Each time Walesa dispelled a crisis, he lost a bit of his support. Still, while the delegates were disappointed with Walesa's compromises, his election, narrow though it was, showed that the union still needed him to prevent the final crisis.

The economy went from deterioration to complete collapse in the fall. Poles stood in lines for everything from matches to toothpaste. Most union leaders believed that Solidarity had to cooperate with the government in some form to repair the economy. Even Gwiazda recognized that self-government was too provocative. But the question remained whether the government would relinquish a degree of its power in return for Solidarity's support for unpopular measures. Walesa called for a "historic compromise," a triple agreement in which the party, the church, and Solidarity would share power on a Committee for National Salvation.

Walesa thought the triple agreement could only take shape if Solidarity showed its willingness to quell strikes that contributed to the economy's decline. In October, Walesa asked Solidarity's National Committee to call for an end to wildcat strikes. When the committee refused, Walesa announced that he was flying to Warsaw for a meeting with General Jaruzelski and Cardinal Jozef Glemp, the new Polish primate. The committee protested, but Walesa made it clear he was not asking for its approval, much less its permission. Gwiazda denounced Walesa as "a vain fool" and "a blockhead." But Walesa hoped he could negotiate the triple agreement at the meeting in Warsaw, and he went despite the National Committee's objections.

If this stage had to end (as it did), I wanted to learn as much as possible, right up to the last minute—learn about democracy, the art of negotiation, and all those areas which, for thirty-five years, had been closed to us, or with which we ourselves had failed to grapple.

—LECH WALESA
on the conflicts between
Solidarity and the Polish
government in 1981

Solidarity holds its first National Congress in Gdansk in September 1981. Meanwhile, Jaruzelski warned that if Solidarity did not moderate its policies the government would promptly take measures to curb the union's "excesses" by force.

Walesa arrived for the November 4 meeting accompanied by Cardinal Glemp. Relations between the church and Solidarity had grown so chilly there was even a debate about whether Glemp and Walesa should ride in the same car. Jaruzelski greeted them with a bright smile, but Walesa was tense as he got out of the primate's car. Jaruzelski proposed a Front for National Agreement, representing seven institutions, most of them controlled by the party. Solidarity could not lend its support to any reform program developed by a committee in which it had only one vote in seven, and Walesa rejected the proposal. The meeting ended only with an agreement for further negotiations.

The outcome left Walesa with nothing to show for his defiance of the National Committee, and he returned to Gdansk groping for something positive to say about the meeting. But the committee, with Gwiazda as acting chairman, had already voted for a general strike within three months if the negotiations failed. Walesa criticized the committee for seeking a confrontation, and Gwiazda and 14 members of the National Committee resigned.

The government continued to negotiate with Solidarity but stalled on the union's demands while the authorities were preparing to break Solidarity once and for all. On November 24, Jaruzelski met with Soviet marshal Viktor Kulikov. On November 28, the party asked the parliament for an Emergency Powers Bill. Days later the government presented an economic reform program completely ignoring Solidarity's self-government proposals. On December 2, Walesa declared "a state of extreme emergency."

As government pressure mounted, Walesa began to examine his options. He could not accept the government's proposal for the Front for National Agreement; it would only water down union proposals until they were unrecognizable. If the government crushed the union, Walesa could resign as chairman and reestablish the union after the authorities had done their handiwork. His advisers dissuaded him from this. Both options meant abandoning his comrades to one degree or another, and Walesa had no intention of doing so. Still, he was desperate to salvage the situation.

In the end, he decided he had no other choice than solidarity with his union comrades. He tried to heal the breaches in Solidarity at a National Committee meeting on December 3. The members were determined to take a strong stand against the government, and Walesa went along with them. Walesa still favored a compromise, but he believed he would be held responsible for any split in the union. "I became the most radical of the radicals," he later recalled. The committee issued a statement denouncing the government for using negotiations merely "as a screen" to hide plans "to attack the union." The committee threatened a 24-hour general strike if parliament enacted the Emergency Powers Bill. On December 6, the state radio broadcast statements from the meeting carefully edited to suggest that Solidarity was plotting to overthrow the government. "Confrontation is inevitable and it will happen," Walesa was heard to say.

> *Mr. Walesa, I look upon you as the liberator of the Polish workers and farmers. I look upon you as a Great National Hero, Mr. Walesa.*
> —from a letter written to Walesa

Walesa was not wrong in saying that confrontation was clearly in the cards, but the tape suggested that he was hoping for it. Walesa had sought to avoid this confrontation for a year. He had let his frustration run away with him just this once, and now the government was using it as a pretext to force the final showdown Walesa had tried to prevent.

On December 11, Walesa opened a National Committee meeting stating, "I declare with my full authority that we are for agreement . . . we do not want any confrontation. The National Agreement must become a reality." The committee endorsed a general strike for December 17. While the debates continued on into the night, messages came in from around the country reporting unusual troop movements and police raids against Solidarity offices. Nervous debates continued in the National Committee. A new resolution was adopted calling for a referendum on whether the authorities were "fit to govern." If the vote was no, the union declared, Solidarity would form a provisional government. By 12:30 A.M. the government had cut off all communications to Gdansk. "Now you've got what you've been looking for," Walesa said angrily. The meeting had come to an end, and so, too, had Poland's 500 days of Solidarity. Walesa went home and waited for the police.

A triumphant Walesa is carried by his fellow workers after being elected chairman of Solidarity at the union's first National Congress. Though the atmosphere at the congress was one of jubilation, Solidarity was deadlocked with the government on the issues most critical to the union's future.

7

Martial Law

Until the night of December 11, Poles still thought that if anyone took military action against Solidarity, it would be the Russian, not the Polish, army. But when the telex machines stopped clattering during Solidarity's National Committee meeting, communications were cut all over Poland, Polish tanks moved into Warsaw, and troops put up roadblocks around major cities. By 3:00 A.M. on December 12, police had arrested thousands of Solidarity activists. At 6:00 A.M., General Jaruzelski went on television to announce that the army had taken over Poland. "The adventurists," he said, referring to Solidarity, "must have their hands tied, before they push the homeland into the abyss of fratricide." Announcers read martial law decrees banning public meetings. Unions and student groups were "suspended." All mail would be censored. Factory workers who disobeyed military discipline could be killed.

All humanity's desire for peace argues for an end to the state of martial law in Poland.
—POPE JOHN PAUL II
in a letter to General
Wojciech Jaruzelski

A woman is apprehended by Polish police in 1981. In December of that year, Solidarity called for a referendum on Communist rule and Poland's ties to the Soviet Union. In response, Jaruzelski declared martial law: He set up a military governing council and had thousands of Solidarity leaders and supporters arrested, including Walesa.

Several Solidarity activists escaped the police, but not Walesa. Jerzy Kolodziejski, governor of the Gdansk region, came to Walesa's apartment soon after he returned from the National Committee meeting. He asked Walesa to go to Warsaw to meet with General Jaruzelski, but Walesa refused. When the governor returned, he was no longer asking Walesa to go to Warsaw — he was ordering him to go. Kolodziejski offered to go with Walesa as a show of good faith, but Walesa told the governor to go home. "I have the feeling that you're going to be transferred at some point yourself," Walesa said.

Jaruzelski asked Walesa to appeal for calm on national television, but Walesa refused. He was taken to a villa outside Warsaw. The government tried many times to get Walesa to support martial law in return for his release, but he would not.

Danuta was nervous when she visited her husband shortly after his arrest, but she found him in

A phalanx of Polish military police form a blockade during the 1981 imposition of martial law. After Jaruzelski announced that the army was taking over the country, factory workers, shipyard workers, and miners throughout Poland organized strikes and demonstrations to protest the government action.

good spirits. He assured her that Solidarity, not the government, was in control, but he only said that because he thought the authorities might be eavesdropping. He wanted to show them that his spirit had not been broken and that martial law had not defeated Solidarity.

Walesa smuggled out appeals asking Poles to resist martial law. The government had not outlawed Solidarity, and Walesa hoped to reach an agreement to save the union. Stanislaw Ciosek, head of the government unions, began visiting Walesa. Ciosek hinted that such an accord was possible, but only if Solidarity expelled certain leaders, including some of his moderate advisers. Walesa had no intention of helping the government discredit his comrades. Still, he did not want to reject the possibility of an agreement. He told Ciosek that he could agree to nothing without meeting with Solidarity leaders first.

A hooded Solidarity supporter prints an antigovernment pamphlet in the winter of 1982. During the period of martial law in Poland, Solidarity was, to a large extent, forced underground: Solidarity meetings were held secretly, and union leaders smuggled messages out of their jail cells.

Two days later, the authorities moved Walesa to a hunting lodge in Arlamow, where Poland's rulers entertained themselves with parties, Western movies, and young women. By keeping Walesa at Arlamow, the government implied he was enjoying all these privileges. Conditions there were not as harsh as those at the internment camps where most Solidarity activists were held. The government tempted Walesa with small favors but punished him at the same time. He was held in a small room, not a cell, and he could listen to the radio; he was allowed visitors but was watched constantly by armed guards; he was given regular meals but fed the same food for days on end. Walesa would often switch plates with his guards, telling them, "If they want to poison someone, I'd rather it be you."

The authorities dropped more hints that Solidarity could be saved. Jaruzelski sent the pope a message offering to negotiate with Walesa through the church. Walesa insisted that two of his advisers be included in the discussions. The church, however, like the government, considered them dangerous radicals, and Walesa agreed to pick more obscure advisers. In the end, the promise of talks came to nothing. Walesa concluded that the government was intent on dismantling the union, and he told church officials he would not cooperate with any such effort.

Walesa prepared for a long stay at Arlamow. When guards took away his radio, Danuta smuggled one in for him, and she became his spokesperson during his internment. He often heard her public statements, and he was proud of her courage. The police could have arrested her at any moment, but she still spoke out defiantly to Western reporters and underground papers.

Public support for Solidarity and Walesa remained strong. Underground activists kept Solidarity alive. At a mass in Warsaw, Poles revised the words of the national anthem to show their support for Walesa. "Lead us, Walesa, from the sea-coast to Silesia," they sang, "Solidarity will rise again and be victorious." Danuta gave birth to her seventh child in January. Walesa was not allowed to attend the christening, but 50,000 Poles did attend in one of the biggest demonstrations under martial law.

The resistance to martial law gave Walesa hope that Solidarity would survive, but by the fall, his internment was beginning to wear him down. Guards told him he would be released if he wrote to Jaruzelski, but Walesa rejected the suggestion.

Solidarity's underground leaders called for a massive protest against martial law on November 11, 1982. Walesa feared that the police would prevent the demonstration by arresting underground activists. With the demonstration only a few days away, he wrote to Jaruzelski: "It seems to me that the time has come to clarify some issues and to work for an agreement." He signed the letter "Lech Walesa, Corporal."

Walesa was released four days later. Many activists criticized Walesa for knuckling under to Jaruzelski. By signing the letter "Corporal," Walesa seemed to suggest that he was a loyal soldier in Jaruzelski's army. Poles, however, were delighted by Walesa's release. A banner hanging from his apartment building proclaimed, WE WANT ONLY YOU AND SOLIDARITY.

Martial law had stripped Walesa of his power. The union he had led was now underground, and the government ignored him. Jaruzelski never even replied to Walesa's request for a meeting. Walesa had spent little time with his family since August 1980. Now he had plenty of time to renew relationships with his seven children. Walesa was proud to see his older sons becoming activists, talking about replacing the director of their school. Walesa had often taken Danuta for granted, too, and returned from Arlamow with a new admiration for her. She had been a full-time parent and an opposition leader, two things Walesa had never managed to do at the same time. "Danuta is more of a hero than I am," he often said.

The authorities had driven Solidarity underground, but the union stood for values that continued to exist in the hearts of ordinary Poles. Walesa believed that as long as Poles lived by those values, Solidarity would continue to exist in spirit until it

> *Mr. Walesa, you'll never be a good politician. Do you know why? Because you're afraid of bloodshed.*
> —Solidarity leaders, to Lech Walesa

A May Day demonstration in 1982. Demonstrations such as this one — and Solidarity itself — were banned by the government that year. Still, the union sustained its momentum by the unwavering determination and commitment of the workers and their leaders.

could reemerge as a union. He assembled a group of advisers at the end of 1982 to help him decide how best to prepare for Solidarity's rebirth. Walesa was so popular the government could not arrest him again without risking protests at home and harsh criticism from abroad. He had freedoms few Poles enjoyed. Using his home as a headquarters, he gave interviews to Western journalists, and he called on the government to release all those arrested during martial law. He emphasized that Solidarity had to be permitted to operate, and he was willing to open a dialogue with the government.

By March 1983, Walesa had grown frustrated with this approach. The government ignored his appeals, and he feared he would jeopardize his place in the opposition if he did not put more pressure on the government. The government was prosecuting several Solidarity leaders, and Walesa traveled around Poland to speak out in their support. The large crowds that greeted Walesa at the trials reminded him of the strike at the Lenin Shipyard.

The underground had grown to several thousand by the spring of 1983. It even had a leadership group, called the Temporary Coordinating Committee (TKK). Walesa had kept his distance from the underground since his release. He believed it showed Poles were still willing to defy the government, and it also maintained a link between Solidarity and the public. Still, he feared the government would use any show of support for the underground as a pretext to avoid reforms. But Walesa agreed to meet with the TKK to show he supported the underground even if he did not intend to join it himself. He and the TKK developed an elaborate plan, Operation Smoke Screen, to make sure the police would not follow him to the meeting. The plan went off without a hitch. Walesa spent three days with underground leaders and left the meeting impressed by the network they had established.

Perhaps to cut down on his opposition activities, the authorities allowed Walesa to return to work at the Lenin Shipyard in late April. In a small shop, Walesa repaired the bulldozers he had used so often to speak to the workers during the August strike. At the end of his first day, workers lined up to shake hands and express their confidence in him.

The government finally lifted martial law in July. All but 60 detainees were released. Poland was no longer under the direct rule of a military junta. Yet many oppressive laws remained in place. Solidarity remained suspended. Poles could not hold public meetings without permission. Dressed in a Solidarity T-shirt, Walesa denounced the new laws, and the government stepped up its propaganda campaign against him. A television documentary claimed Walesa was a paid agent of foreign powers.

In October, Walesa was awarded the Nobel Peace Prize, and 2,000 people gathered outside Walesa's apartment, chanting "WA-LE-SA! SO-LI-DAR-NOSC! LE-SZEK!" Walesa's apartment was filled with journalists, camera crews, and well-wishers. The award was a personal triumph that gave Poles hope, but the government still persecuted Walesa's comrades. Walesa thanked the supporters outside his apartment. "Everyone is pleased," he said, "but not all are equally so. Many people are still in prison, many have been thrown out of their jobs. Many nameless people have deserved this award, and I feel ashamed that at present I am so powerless to help them."

Poland . . . will never perish.
—LECH WALESA

Lech Walesa is moved by the news that he has been chosen to receive the Nobel Peace Prize in October 1983. Afraid that the government would attempt to block his return to Poland, Walesa sent Danuta to Sweden to accept the award on his behalf.

Walesa decided he would not go to Oslo, Norway, to accept the award. He believed the government might not allow him to return to Poland. He also did not want to be honored in the West while his comrades remained in jail. He decided to send Danuta to accept the award for him. Western governments had stopped all loans to Poland in protest against martial law. Solidarity welcomed the sanctions as a show of support, but Poland's faltering economy made life a daily struggle for Poles and undermined their will to resist the government. In his Nobel Prize speech, Walesa would ask the West to lift the sanctions.

Danuta went to Oslo in December, while her husband watched television coverage of her trip with a twinge of jealousy, seeing all the attention she received. She had been nervous before leaving for Oslo, but she was calm and dignified accepting the award. Walesa later said he "fell in love with her all over again" watching her accept the prize. In Walesa's acceptance speech, read by Bogdan Cywinski, one of the experts who advised Solidarity during the shipyard strike, Walesa emphasized that Poles remained committed to creating a more democratic Poland through nonviolence. "We must not close any doors or do anything that would block the road to an understanding. But we must remember that only a peace built on the foundations of justice and a moral order can be a lasting one," he said.

The prestige of the Nobel Prize gave Walesa more protection from the authorities. Walesa began to speak more frequently about the future of the opposition. He said Poles had to prepare for the time when the working class would rise in revolt again. Solidarity had reached a new stage. Poles could no longer let leaders decide what kind of society they wanted and how to create it. Workers had to decide how to run their factories, doctors their hospitals, and students their universities. "We have been humiliated and insulted," he told 1,500 Poles at a church outside Gdansk. "Let us all see to it that we are humiliated no more. . . . Let everyone find the truth about this country in the context of his or her own family or factory."

By 1984 the government seemed to have adopted a two-pronged strategy. It harassed the opposition but held out the hope that cooperation would lead to reform. Jaruzelski began to loosen the hold of central planners over the economy. The government announced local elections. If they succeeded, imprisoned Solidarity leaders would be released. Although the elections gave voters a choice, the government still chose the candidates. On the recommendation of Walesa and other opposition leaders, an estimated 10 million Poles boycotted the elections, a vote of no-confidence for the government.

The government said the elections showed Solidarity's lack of support, but events soon proved otherwise. The government released the Solidarity leaders who had remained in prison. Many people feared they might break with Solidarity, but one by one they returned to the fold. On May 1, the government celebrated May Day. Walesa and 200 workers infiltrated the parade, flashing V-for-victory signs as they passed the reviewing stand where government officials watched the procession. In October 1984 the security police murdered Father Jerzy Popieluszko, an outspoken Solidarity supporter. At Father Popieluszko's funeral, it was as if Poland had gone backward in time to August 1980. Solidarity

An elated crowd of workers cheers Walesa as he returns to work at the Lenin Shipyard in the spring of 1983. Though the government had fired Walesa for his political activities, he was allowed to return to work because the government considered the numerous demonstrations demanding his reinstatement a menace to the state.

The funeral of Father Jerzy Popieluszko, clergyman and Solidarity activist. In October 1984, the police killed Father Popieluszko for his outspoken opposition to the Polish government. Walesa said of the murder, "Here is proof that . . . terror and blackmail [are] an integral part of the methods of political repression practiced against the citizens of Poland."

banners flapped in the wind. A loudspeaker announced the arrival of "the National Committee of Solidarity, with Lech Walesa." Walesa believed the reaction to Father Popieluszko's death showed the opposition's strength despite the government's attempts to beat and cajole Poland into submission. "I felt the crowd swell with confidence," Walesa later recalled, "I felt their faith in moral values strengthened, their faith in the necessity of realizing these values in society. The more this conviction spread, the stronger would be our defense against evil, against the pitfalls of chaos and despair."

The murder of Father Popieluszko was the most dramatic example of the government crackdown on opposition activity. A thriving underground culture had grown up since martial law. Banned theater companies continued to perform, and journalists wrote for 500 underground publications. Students studied with banned teachers in classes that moved from one apartment to another, called "Flying Universities." In the fall of 1984, the government began to crack down on this independent culture. Several Solidarity leaders were jailed in 1985.

After Father Popieluszko's murder, Walesa told an underground paper that the government's propaganda had become "a ruthless struggle against any reconciliation or agreement. We are faced with propaganda terrorism." The police brought Walesa in for questioning several times.

A new Soviet leader, Mikhail S. Gorbachev, came to power in the spring of 1985. The Soviet Union was suffering from the same economic problems that plagued Poland. The Communist party's rigid control over the Soviet economy had proved unable to satisfy public demand for better food and housing, just as Poland's Communist party had failed to satisfy the Polish people's economic aspirations. Gorbachev encouraged the Soviet press to become more open and critical, particularly of the economy. He encouraged Russians to open their own businesses and find new ways to make state-run factories more productive and prodded Eastern European countries to adopt similar policies. The Soviet Union, always the major obstacle to political

and economic reform in Poland, was now encouraging it.

Spurred on by Gorbachev, Jaruzelski took steps in 1986 that Solidarity activists believed might lead to real reform. Official newspapers began publishing information about the sorry state of the economy, a key Solidarity demand in 1981. In September the government announced it would release all political prisoners. "No one in our country is or will be discriminated against for his or her convictions," Jaruzelski claimed. He also invited intellectuals and church leaders to join a "Social Consultative Council" to advise him on political and economic reform. Jaruzelski took these steps because he wanted Western governments to give Poland new loans and because by appearing willing to discuss reforms, he hoped to deepen divisions between the church, which favored cooperation with the regime, and Solidarity, which was divided on this matter.

Still, most Solidarity leaders believed Jaruzelski's main purpose was economic. Trucks and trains rusted away unused because of a spare parts shortage. Many factories lay idle. Jaruzelski also seemed to see that economic and political reform went hand in hand, that Poles would not work harder unless they had more say over how Poland was governed.

Jaruzelski (wearing glasses) meets with Soviet leader Mikhail Gorbachev in Moscow on April 21, 1987. In the 1980s, Gorbachev instituted policies aimed at restructuring the Soviet economy and created a more open forum for public debate of social issues in the Soviet Union. By the end of the decade, it remained to be seen what those reforms might mean for Poland.

An elderly woman sells poultry in Warsaw's Rozycki Bazaar, where, during the 1987 meat-rationing program, Poles could buy meat from private individuals to supplement their official monthly allotment. In the late 1980s, Poland's economy continued to buckle under the strain of a striking labor force, dire food shortages, and government policies with little or no public support.

Solidarity began to reassess Jaruzelski. "I must admit that in the past I had a very low opinion of Jaruzelski and the people around him," Walesa said. "But having gotten to know them, I've changed my mind. They are first-class professionals, not to be underrated."

Jaruzelski's new program intrigued Solidarity leaders. But it also divided them. Many, including Walesa, believed they now had the perfect opportunity to bring Solidarity back into the open. Some people wanted to maintain the Solidarity underground in case they had overestimated Jaruzelski's good intentions. Others wanted to form a group of intellectuals independent of the opposition to negotiate with Jaruzelski about Solidarity's status. In September, Solidarity formed a Provisional Council headed by Walesa. A similar council was established in Warsaw. Solidarity was still outlawed, so this was a risky maneuver. The council decided not to dissolve the underground in case Jaruzelski arrested council members. The council and the underground leadership merged in October 1987.

In November 1987 the government asked Poles to vote on a government program for "radical economic recovery" even if it required a "difficult" three-year period of "rapid changes." The regime also asked Poles if they supported political reforms aimed at "strengthening self-government, extending the rights of citizens and increasing their participation" in running the country. The referendum was vague, to be sure. But Poles saw that the government was asking them whether they were willing to endure sharp price increases to improve the economy. In the past, the government simply raised prices without even telling them, much less asking them whether they approved. Now, the government was asking for their approval. Still, the government did not specify what economic measures it planned to take. Nor did it say exactly what political reforms it had in mind. Furthermore, Poles could not cast their ballots freely as long as they feared voting against the government could lead to reprisals. Solidarity called for a boycott. One-third of all Polish voters did not take part in the referendum. Only 44 percent voted in favor of the government's economic program, and only 46 percent supported the government's political reforms, an embarrassing defeat. The government had sought the public's approval and lost. Yet Jaruzelski could also say nearly half the population supported him.

The government went ahead with its program. On December 15, it announced that prices would rise 27 percent in 1988. Though price increases had sparked rebellions in 1970, 1976, and 1980, the February 1988 increases took effect, and Polish workers seemed to accept them at first. But when prices were increased in April, the strikes the government feared erupted in full force. On April 25, workers at Nowa Huta, the largest industrial plant in Poland, went on strike, demanding wage increases and the reinstatement of four Solidarity members who had been fired for union activities. Workers in arms plants near Krakow took these demands one step further, insisting the government legalize Solidarity.

Solidarity had called for nationwide protests on May 1 to coincide with official May Day parades. With the protests approaching, the idea spread that a growing strike wave could topple the government — a repeat of events in 1956, 1970, and 1980. May Day protests took place in 12 cities, including Warsaw and Gdansk, where Walesa spoke to several thousand people at a rally. Walesa called for a nationwide "day of action" but insisted workers decide for themselves whether they should show their support for strikers in Nowa Huta and elsewhere with strikes of their own. "It's up to you to decide what to do," he said. "If you have an army, General Lech Walesa is at your disposal."

Workers at the Lenin Shipyard decided to call a strike. Walesa spoke at the shipyard gates the evening of May 2. Walesa's advisers were reluctant to lend his name and prestige to spontaneous strikes whose fate was so uncertain. Walesa said he was neither for nor against the strike but that he would support the workers in the course they had chosen.

The strike harkened back to August 1980 in many ways. Three thousand workers occupied the shipyard, and the main gate was draped with banners and Polish flags. The workers drew up a list of am-

Don't let's look backwards, but forward. This past is in all of us, the real work is before us.
—LECH WALESA

bitious and inspired demands that had gone un-
spoken in the seven years since Solidarity was
crushed. The workers demanded that wages be increased, political prisoners released, and Solidarity
legalized. There were moments of tremendous excitement when workers felt that united once again
they might remake Poland as they had in 1980. On
May 3, Andrzej Gwiazda read out a message from
the strikers at the Lenin works in Nowa Huta to the
workers of the Lenin Shipyard. "One Lenin started
this," he shouted, "and two Lenin's will end it."

But the strike in April 1988 was also very different
from the one in August 1980. Though other yards
sent messages of support to the Lenin Shipyard
workers, very few of them actually went on strike
themselves to show that support. As in 1980, people
gathered around the Lenin Shipyard gates, but this
time there were fewer. Many of those who did not
gather at the gates had taken part in the strikes of
1980 and now believed Solidarity was too radical.
They had fought for Solidarity in 1980 and today
had little to show for it. The majority of them had
families now and were therefore concerned more
with higher wages than with political demands such
as the right to strike and the establishment of independent trade unions. Most of those who did con-
gregate at the shipyard gates came of age during
martial law, a time of dashed hopes and disillusionment. Many of them supported Solidarity but believed it had been too moderate. They were desperate
for change and wanted the movement to be more
confrontational, whereas Walesa considered aggres-
sive confrontation dangerous and potentially self-
defeating.

The differences between the strikes of 1980 and
those of 1988 were also apparent from the change
in Walesa and in the workers' reaction to him. Workers cheered him and climbed up on walls and sheds
to get a better look at him, just as they had in 1980,
but fewer people were impressed by what they saw.
Walesa was older now, and he seemed to have lost
some of his fire. More than a touch of gray was
visible in his mustache, and at his waistline was an
unflattering middle-aged spread. He had developed
back trouble, and he suffered from diabetes.

As Walesa mounted the platform to speak on May 3, a young worker rolled his eyes. "Elegant," he muttered to himself, referring to Walesa's tweed jacket, which clashed with the workers' grimy overalls. Walesa's enthusiasm in 1980 was infectious; now the workers were looking at a tired man who was ready to pass the baton. "You have to create a couple of new Walesas. I did my part. Now I have other things to do." Walesa had told workers in 1980 not to give up until all their demands were met but had always advised restraint. His message was still the same. "If we do not make reforms peacefully and with compromises, then we are threatened with a revolution and a bloody one," he said.

The government's hard line made peaceful compromise impossible. On May 5, the security police stormed Nowa Huta. In Gdansk, police surrounded the shipyard, rhythmically pounding their plastic shields with truncheons to frighten the strikers. Several workers broke under the strain; one even tried to kill himself. Walesa did his best to calm the workers. "You know Solidarity also means watching the guy next to you. You have to look into his eyes. If there's a strange look, you have to ask: Can I help? And you can come to Walesa, pull on his sleeve and say 'Walesa, I have a problem.' We have to carry on, especially now, when things are dangerous." On May 6, the strike ended with no agreement. Calling the decision a truce, not a defeat, Walesa told strikers to go home "with your heads high" before they filed grimly out of the yard carrying a wooden cross and an icon of the Black Madonna.

The government raised prices again in August, and workers again responded with strikes that brought coal mines, factories, and ports, including the Lenin Shipyard, to a standstill. Walesa met with Interior Minister General Czeslaw Kiszczak on August 31. The government agreed to begin round-table discussions with Solidarity, the church, and other social groups on a wide range of issues, including the legalization of Solidarity. Walesa emerged from the meeting calling for an end to all strikes as a show of good faith in preparation for the talks.

The meeting was a major victory for Walesa. After

Workers enter the Lenin Shipyard during a strike in May 1988. As the 1980s drew to a close, Solidarity was very much alive, but it was uncertain how much of a role Walesa would play in the future of the labor movement. Despite the international reputation he had earned for his dedication to the workers' cause, Walesa repeatedly reminded his admiring public, "I am just an ordinary worker."

years of relentless criticism, the government had agreed to begin the talks Solidarity had demanded in 1981 as a prelude to a national accord between the state and society. Still, many oppositionists saw matters differently. To them, Walesa's agreement with the authorities resembled the strikes in 1980 and 1981, when Walesa personally negotiated accords to end strikes without union approval. Also, they pointed out that Walesa's meeting with the government had secured nothing more than a promise to hold more meetings.

Solidarity leaders demanded that their union be legalized prior to any further negotiations, but the government refused. Walesa persuaded the leadership to talk anyway, but before the government could be approached it launched a vicious anti-Solidarity campaign in the press, and Jaruzelski named a fierce Solidarity opponent, Mieczyslaw Rakowski, as his new prime minister. Communication between Solidarity and the government broke down, Poland's economic crisis worsened, and the Polish people, not falling for the government's attempt to discredit Solidarity, rallied around the union leadership.

Then, at a Communist party meeting in January 1989, Jaruzelski took unprecedented steps toward reconciliation. In a shocking speech, he announced his intention to resign unless the party resolved to legalize Solidarity. He pointed to Poland's severe social and economic problems and explained that popular support was necessary if the government was to be effective in such difficult times.

In June, despite ruthless opposition from party hard-liners, elections were held in Poland, and the Communist party was humiliated both by the popular support for Solidarity and the outright rejection of party candidates. Though he remained president, Jaruzelski resigned his post as Communist party leader, and the first noncommunist coalition government in the Soviet bloc was formed in Poland. Public support at the polls put many Solidarity leaders in key political positions: Tadeusz Mazowiecki, one of Walesa's closest advisers, replaced Rakowski as Poland's prime minister; Jacek Kuron became minister of labor; and Adam Michnik was elected to the senate. In addition, Solidarity was granted parliamentary power and a prominent role in determining the country's economic policies. Thus, Walesa would be called on to be a key player in Poland's future.

We are one big family—a world family—and we share a common fate.
—LECH WALESA

What does the future hold for Poland? When the new Polish government took over in 1989, it was faced with a staggering foreign debt of $40 billion and an annual inflation rate of nearly 100 percent. Poland still had not developed any modern technology and was in no position to produce goods that would be marketable abroad. Food, housing, and health care were still scarce and very expensive while wages remained inadequate. In 1989 it seemed that nothing short of a miracle could save Poland from social and economic collapse.

Still, Poles are no strangers to adversity. They have survived a long history of foreign oppression and have repeatedly survived near devastation because of their great inner strength. During the 1980s, the Polish people remained united and hopeful at least to some degree because Walesa and Solidarity provided them with that unity and hope. Though Poland's future is very uncertain, there is little doubt that Walesa and the spirit of Solidarity will inspire Poles for many decades to come.

Further Reading

Ascherson, Neal. *The Polish August: The Self-Limiting Revolution*. New York: Viking Press, 1982.

Ash, Timothy Garton. *The Polish Revolution: Solidarity*. New York: Vintage, 1985.

Brolewicz, Walter. *My Brother, Lech Walesa*. New York: Tribeca, 1983.

Brumberg, Abraham, ed. *Poland: Genesis of A Revolution*. New York: Vintage, 1983.

Craig, Mary. *The Crystal Spirit: Lech Walesa and His Poland*. London: Hodder and Stoughton, 1986.

Dobbs, Michael. *Poland/Solidarity/Walesa*. New York: McGraw-Hill, 1981.

Eringer, Robert. *Strike for Freedom: The Story of Lech Walesa and Polish Solidarity*. New York: Dodd, Mead, 1982.

Gault, Francois. *Walesa*. Paris: Centurion, 1981.

Michnik, Adam. *Letters from Prison and Other Essays*. Berkeley: University of California Press, 1987.

Nowakowski, Marek. *The Canary and Other Tales of Martial Law*. Garden City, NY: Dial Press, 1984.

Singer, Daniel. *The Road to Gdansk: Poland and the USSR*. New York: Monthly Review Press, 1981.

Solidarity Friends & Members. *The Book of Lech Walesa*. New York: Simon & Schuster, 1982.

Touraine, Alain, et al. *Solidarity: Poland 1980–1981*. Cambridge: Cambridge University Press, 1983.

Walesa, Lech. *A Way of Hope*. New York: Holt, Rinehart, & Winston, 1987.

Weschler, Lawrence. *Solidarity: Poland in the Season of Its Passion*. New York: Simon & Schuster, 1982.

Chronology

September 29, 1943	Born Lech Walesa in Popowo, Poland
1945	Polish Communists take power in Warsaw
1967	Walesa takes a job at the Lenin Shipyard
1968	Supports student antigovernment protests
1969	Marries Danuta Golos
1970	Several workers are killed by police during a strike at the Lenin Shipyard
1971	Walesa meets with Polish leader Edward Gierek
1976	Fired for making a speech criticizing Gierek; hired as mechanic for ZREMB building company
1978	Joins Free Trade Unions (FTU); fired from ZREMB for FTU activities
1979	Hired by Elektromontaz engineering company, which soon fired him for speaking at a memorial service for workers killed during the 1970 strike
July 31, 1980	Arrested for political activities and held for 12 hours
August 1980	Declares a strike at the Lenin Shipyard; named head of the Inter-Factory Strike Committee; signs agreement guaranteeing independent trade unions
September 1980	Solidarity establishes headquarters in Gdansk with Walesa as chairman of the Temporary National Committee
November 1980	The government sends Walesa to Warsaw to help contain strikes there
January 1981	Walesa meets with Pope John Paul II in Rome; negotiates agreement with government over a new farmers' union
March 1981	Threatens to resign from the National Committee
October 1981	Elected chairman of Solidarity
December 1981	Arrested when General Wojciech Jaruzelski declares martial law
November 1982	Released from prison
July 21, 1983	Martial law is lifted
1987	Walesa publishes his autobiography, *A Way of Hope*, in the United States
1988	Strikes break out in Nowa Huta and other Polish industrial cities; workers demand wage increases and legalization of Solidarity
1989	Solidarity is legalized; free elections are held in Poland; a coalition government, the first noncommunist government in the Eastern bloc, is formed in Poland

Index

Page numbers in italic refer to photographs.

Tony Kaye is a free-lance writer and a graduate student in history at Columbia University. His work has appeared in *The New Republic, The Nation,* and *Nuclear Times.* He has served as research director of the Democracy Project and as senior staff associate at the New York University Center of War, Peace, and the News Media.

Arthur M. Schlesinger, jr., taught history at Harvard for many years and is currently Albert Schweitzer Professor of the Humanities at City University of New York. He is the author of numerous highly praised works in American history and has twice been awarded the Pulitzer Prize. He served in the White House as special assistant to Presidents Kennedy and Johnson.
